"He's familiar, but at the same time you don't know about his personal life, so you can project onto him what you want him to be. He can be your cute son, the dad you wish you had, your lover, the man who got away, your best buddy. Johnny has made himself into a Rorschach for America."

—Dr. Joyce Brothers

"Johnny Carson has done more to ruin America's love life than anyone else in the country. On any given night that he's hosting *The Tonight Show* there are 10 times more couples watching his monologue than making love."

—Dr. Ruth Westheimer

"I called Johnny a great American institution—like Broadway or baseball or Congress. Johnny said I was doing just fine until I mentioned Congress."

—John McLaughlin

"See, he is not a talk-show host. He is a national institution."

—Peter Jennings

"Johnny Carson is a wonderful guy, very entertaining. I love him, he loves me, he loves you, he's gonna retire, and I knew him well. Goodbye, so long, God bless him. Now he can go on with his tennis."

—Don Rickles

"I think Johnny is truly the best of all of them. You know, Johnny thinks funny. It's not enough to write funny. You've got to think funny."

—Jonathan Winters

"I think Johnny was America's answer to foreplay—he's very American, very topical."

—Joan Collins

"The American people are smart. We often know quality when we see it. The popularity of Carson's unscripted, free-form thinking and his skeptical attitudes toward politicians of all parties say something very healthy about the country."

—Carl Sagan

40 YEARS
AT NIGHT

The story of the TONIGHT SHOW

James Van Hise

Books for the entertainment buyer

PIONEER

Library of Congress Cataloging-in-Publication Data
Scott Nance—
    Forty Years at Night: The Story of the Tonight Show

    1.   Forty Years at Night: The Story of the Tonight Show (television)
  I. Title

Published by Pioneer Books, Inc., 5715 N. Balsam Rd., Las Vegas, NV, 89130.

First Printing, 1992

FOR ANDY...PEACE

The author wishes to thank all of the people who helped make this book possible, including the NBC network. Special thanks go to Mr. Jack Paar and Mr. Steve Allen and his staff, without whose help this would not have been possible.

SCOTT NANCE has contributed regularly to a variety of entertainment magazines including CLASSIC ROCK, ROCK and SONG HITS,, and numerous other music and nostalgia television publications. In addition, he is the author of ZZ TOP: RECYCLING THE BLUES and THE NEW KIDS ON THE BLOCK, also by Pioneer Books.

Introduction

The challenges will be many as Jay Leno replaces Johnny Carson as host of *The Tonight Show*. Carson has built a late-night empire over the past thirty years, reigning as the undisputed "King of Midnight." For three decades, Carson has been the "national comedian," his monologues and the antics with his guests the subject of conversation the next day by young and old, men and women, rich and poor. As his former manager once said, "He's loved in all fifty states." That admiration has made him the most watched entertainer in history, having introduced thousands of guests and been on the air for even more thousands of hours of television. Johnny Carson sitting behind his desk at that microphone has become a unique piece of contemporary Americana.

There's more to Carson than an impish grin and a Midwestern wit. Off-camera, he is a demanding perfectionist who expects nothing less of his staff or himself. Having Johnny Carson for a boss is a lot of work, even for Carson himself. "What has happened before the curtain rises is about as low-key as a subway station during an air raid," admitted Craig Tennis, former head talent coordinator on *The Tonight Show*. Intricate and intense work goes into the program; it is not the gala it appears to be to the studio audience or the millions of viewers watching from their couches or beds each night.

"Instead of an intimate party going on back there, it's a frenzied workshop, glorifying the power of suggestion over truth—it is, in other words, a show. An illusion," said Tennis, frankly. "What's more, the man we seem to know so well is not only the illusion-maker, he is the illusion itself." The basic illusion is that on the show, Carson is gregarious, outgoing, but away from his audience, he is quiet, reserved, and profoundly private.

Carson is at work from the moment he awakes. He reads the newspaper and watches the morning news programs, searching current events for just the right joke or jab for the evening's monologue, a monologue that has become a key political barometer. Carson might spend part of the morning playing tennis at his Bel Air home with friends such as Steve Lawrence or Ricardo Montalban.

He isn't due at the NBC studio in Burbank until later that afternoon. He goes back to work, alone and secluded in his office-cabana built near his house. The cabana is complete with a seven-foot television screen, a VCR, and a lone barber-like chair. There are also a few toys, such as Carson's drum set. But Carson doesn't play too much, he seems much more content quietly working on his show. During the morning, he's in frequent contact with Freddie de Cordova, the long time *Tonight Show* producer, checking on guests and the writers' material.

Around one-thirty, Carson drives himself in his Corvette to the NBC studio. Once his in office, he goes through all of the material the talent coordinators have given him to prepare him for that evening's guests. The talent coordinators are the ones who actually solicit the guests, and furnish Carson with background on suggested questions for each. He reads a sampling of the show's mail, and then goes through the monologue material and whatever skits the writers have written, such as the classic Carnac he Magnificent or Aunt Blabby bits. If he likes any of those, he'll go with them. He puts the finishing touches on his monologue. He meets with de Cordova at four, meets with his director, finishes wardrobe and make-up, and is ready to go on at five-thirty. "It's worked so far—but God knows why, so let's not mess with it," Carson once said.

It all runs like the proverbial well-oiled machine, but day in and day out and it is grueling. Once the insides of *The Tonight*

Show are exposed, one gains a little better understanding, and a greater dose of sympathy for Carson's extended vacations.

The all-too-familiar theme comes up courtesy of Doc Severinsen and the NBC orchestra, McMahon announces the legendary, "Heeere's Johnny . . . ," and Carson pops out from behind the curtain already smiling, and the illusion is complete. It's the method behind th*Tonight Show* we all have come to not only love, but to expect. After all, after we tune in to the same entertainment practically every weeknight for three decades, we've gotten used to it.

Retirement changes all that for both Carson and *The Tonight Show*. After Carson announced his departure, McMahon, Severinsen, and producer de Cordova followed suit. Jay Leno will find his own crew, will work out his own routine, his own well-oiled machine, his own *Tonight Show*. The success of *The Tonight Show* rests on the central success of the host. "I'm me on *The Tonight Show*," Carson observed, and Jay Leno will be Jay Leno.

This transition isn't as alien to the program as most believe. *The Tonight Show* is older than Johnny Carson's thirty years as host; it goes back another decade, almost to the birth of television itself. It began as a live show broadcast every night from sophisticated New York City. Carson was the third host of the show—he had to break himself in, find his own style, and in the process made *The Tonight Show* his own. Carson replaced Jack Paar, host from '57 to '62, who Carson himself believed would be irreplaceable. Paar, in turn, had to supplant popular funnyman Steve Allen, who originated the program for NBC in 1951.

Each host has imprinted the show with his own personality. In the process, each has expanded the very nature of television. Steve Allen took a medium with no expectations in the early '50s and accomplished a feat no one believed possible, he got Americans to stay awake past eleven o'clock at night to watch television. After Allen left for greener pastures, Jack Paar, the original TV rebel, came aboard and made TV spontaneous, controversial. Carson and his producers actually developed the format seen today, a concept copied not only by late-night competitors but by programs at every hour of the day.

Jay Leno will make his own contribution in the months, years, perhaps decades, ahead. Steve Allen, who later came back to the show as one of Carson's many guest hosts over the years, commented, *"The Tonight Show* could be run by a chimpanzee and people would continue to watch out of habit." Today, when *The Tonight Show* faces stiff competition from imitators on a regular basis, what Allen fails to note is that chimp has to have something special.

Steve Allen: A Disc Jockey for Television

"She was one of those typical Greenwich, Connecticut matrons—proper, a trifle brittle, well-educated, sporting the tailored look of Peck & Peck, the fashion house," later recounted one television critic. "She was an expert on house pets and had brought a magnificent model home: the exterior was an exact replica of a Victorian house. Several of her pets were inside, some playing and some sleeping."

The camera came to settle on that model house, and Steve Allen asked the woman, "What is this thing?"

"Oh, that," she responded casually, "that's a cathouse." That response touched off laughter throughout the studio, and in host Allen himself. Former *Tonight!* bandleader Skitch Henderson observed, "Steve Allen could do an hour and a half on a gag like that." In the 1950s, with his new free-form television show, it seemed like entertainer Steve Allen—the original King of the Night—almost did just that sometimes.

There was just something captivating about a live show from electric New York City that would keep people up until one in the morning. And Steve Allen's charm and wit were behind it all. He came to *Tonight!* having mastered radio ad-lib and with a heritage in vaudeville.

Allen's parents, Billy and Belle Allen were both vaudeville performers, joining professionally as they joined matrimonially; on stage, they put on a comedy act, Billy playing Belle's straight man. But young Steve's childhood was not full of laughs, even if he had been befriended as a boy by the legendary Mae West. Steve was his parents' only child, born the day after Christmas, 1921. He later said his birth was like "a forgotten Christmas present."

Billy and Belle were too busy doing shows out on the road to spend much with their son. When young Steve was sick, his parents left him in a San Francisco hospital while they moved to another town to perform. Steve's Aunt Rose reunited the boy with his parents several months later. The young boy's life took a more tragic turn when his father died when he was only eighteen months old.

Belle kept working the vaudeville circuit while bringing her son Steve along in tow. "I can dimly remember waking up alone in the middle of the night in various hotel rooms, wondering where I was and wondering where my mother was," Steve remembered. "Sometimes I would get up, get dressed, and go out into the night looking for her."

As Steve grew to school age, Belle began to leave him with members of her family, but they too put limits on Steve. After a time, Steve settled in Chicago, but still wasn't happy. "When we rode on streetcars, my aunts would force me to take the only vacant seat while they stood up. I was quite tall for my age and was greatly embarrassed. When I was twelve I unconsciously began trying to break away. The corner drugstore became my favorite hangout. My aunts demanded that I get to bed early to protect my health, and if I stayed out, they fought furiously over who was to blame."

With $7 in his pocket, young Steve ran away, ending up at his Aunt Nora's home in California. In California, Steve finished a year of high school before returning to family in Chicago. Upon his arrival, he began submitting his poetry to the Chicago *Tribune*, and more importantly to his career, found himself with a piano at home which he began to experiment with. "Life looked pretty rosy, I recall," Steve remembered, "with my stuff breaking in the Chicago papers, living with Mother and Aunt Maggie, having my own piano, making a few dollars each week by playing high school dance jobs, and my shyness drying up a little. What more could a guy want?"

What more? Possibly a job that would send him on the route to stardom. When Allen was a junior in high school, his asthma forced him to move to a warmer, drier place. He and his mother packed up, took a train to Phoenix and found a place to live across from Steve's new high school, where he joined the school paper and received his diploma. He entered Drake University on a scholarship, transferred to Arizona State Teachers College a year later, and finally dropped out to take a job at radio station KOY.

At KOY, Allen was a general announcer, but he also wrote news stories, scripted a soap opera called *Love Story Time* and played records. During World War II, Allen left the station for a time to enter the service, stationed in California. Duty proved too stressful for his asthma and he was discharged, but not before he was married.

Allen and his new wife returned to Arizona and he returned to KOY, then left KOY for a late night disc-jockey job in California at KNX radio. There he began the improvised comedy that later made him a hit on *Tonight!* KNX management wasn't keen on Allen's comedy, and ordered him to play records. In his free-wheeling style, Allen read the memo on the air and droves of fans came to his rescue, demanding that Allen be allowed to continue his winning comedy. DJ Allen got another, more sheepish memo from the station executives, reading: "Well, you win. Go ahead and talk, but play a little music, okay?"

Allen seemed right on track; his hilarious comedy got the attention of talent agent Jules Green. Green soon got Allen off radio and into the burgeoning medium of television. On TV, Green placed Allen on the game show *What's My Line?* where the comedian coined the now-cliche phrase, "Is it bigger than a breadbox?" Allen also never gave up the piano and developed into quite a composer. With that experience, he also hosted a composers' showcase called *Songs for Sale*. But Green very much wanted to Allen out of the basement of daytime and up to more exposure at night.

His big break came when Ted Cott from the local NBC affiliate offered him the chance to host a local late night show sponsored by Knickerbocker beer. The offer came to Allen with this condition: "I'm not going to pay Steve one penny over $1,500 a week." Both Allen and Green leapt at the chance, Green explaining that for Steve, "I was prepared to take $1,000."

Like its KNX radio predecessor, the local television *Steve Allen Show* was a smash success; so much so, in fact, that it attracted the attention of Pat Weaver, an NBC network executive.

2

America Tonight!

In the early '50s, NBC had launched its first late-night venture, a live variety program called *Broadway Open House*. Sylvester "Pat" Weaver, the maverick creative programming executive who is better known today as the father of actress Sigourney Weaver, had seen a vast potential in advertising revenue in the late night hours. He had tapped a comic named Creesh Hornsby to host the live show based from Manhattan, but Hornsby died in a tragic accident before the debut. For a time, other comedians filled in temporarily, most notably Jerry Lewis who picked fun at sponsor Anchor Hocking's "unbreakable" crockery. He was finally able to break a goblet on the air.

The show needed a stable anchor, a permanent host. NBC contacted a nightclub comedian named Jerry Lester, who at first was reluctant to continue to work in television. Lester's agent coaxed him, and finally Lester asked, "How much do you pay?"

NBC replied with, "What do you want?"

Lester turned to his wife and asked, "How much does that stole you want cost?" That amount is what Lester asked for in salary. For his debut, Lester went on as he put it, "with no make-up, and no jokes." In a format similar to later *Tonight* incarnations, Lester was assisted by an announcer, Wayne Howell, and an orchestra led by bandleader Milton DeLugg. *Broadway Open House* was vaudeville on television.

Both the audience and the executives loved it. Lester agreed to continue *Broadway Open House* for another thirteen

weeks. He would do the Monday, Wednesday, and Friday shows, and Morey Amsterdam—who later gained comic immortality on *The Dick Van Dyke Show*—would cover Tuesdays and Thursdays. One television critic put it this way, "Amsterdam was good, but basically, Morey's output was a letdown after Jerry, and he became kind of a bookmark holding the television page until Lester returned the following night."

Lester's programs were a true phenomenon. NBC wanted a commitment from their star that he would continue *Broadway Open House*. He agreed to another five weeks. "This is the spot every artist should find himself in. I really dealt," he later recalled.

Lester also brought in more characters, most notably a "dumb blonde" named Dagmar. Steve Allen later called Dagmar "a sort of cross between Dolly Parton and Victoria Jackson." She started out just sitting silently with the orchestra with the sign "Girl Singer" on her stool. Then she became a speaking cast member.

"We worked from a script about two pages long, double-spaced, with two lines to explain each sketch," Lester explained. "We created a door gag to open each segment."

TV critic Jack Gould reviewed the program this way, "As a matter of fact, *Broadway Open House* frequently is so beyond credulity that it exercises an almost hypnotic effect on the viewer. It is a sort of theatrical counterpart of a wrestling match. In the morning you may wonder why you lost sleep over it, but chances are you will watch it again."

Amidst success, trouble brewed on the set; creative differences split the cast, and Jerry Lester left the show. Amsterdam's appearances were canceled. NBC tried to hold on with other comedians, but none were as successful as Lester. *Broadway Open House* left the air August 23, 1951.

Pat Weaver seized upon Steve Allen's local program as the logical network entry into late night. It was a little more involved than Weaver first anticipated. NBC wanted ownership; Allen, and his agent Jules Green, insisted they retain ownership. Green and feared that if NBC owned the show, the network would have the ability to override Allen creatively. Green and Allen were determined to direct the show's creative future.

Green and Allen had reason to be suspicious. NBC had already launched their morning news program, *Today*, and the rumor was that NBC wanted to make Allen's show a lighter version of *Today*, rather than the open-ended variety format Allen wanted. Also, in the move from local to network, NBC retained Allen's director, Dwight Hemion, but did not want to bring along producer Billy Harbach.

Allen felt Harbach was a top-notch producer, but Harbach came off looking foolish because he made speaking mistakes when he had a lot on his mind. Harbach once asked a set designer, "How many feet in a foot?" Harbach was worse with names. At one point, he asked his secretary to call Charton Heston. Instead, he shouted, "Get me—uh—Charleston Huston; er, uh—Charleton Hudson. You know, Chester Moses."

NBC and Weaver wanted a viable late night entry enough to give in to Allen and Green, and RoseMeadow—the Allen and Green corporation—took ownership of the program, which the network called *Tonight!* to counterbalance the earlier *Today*. Allen kept Harbach.

3

America Tonight!

Steve Allen made that all-important jump from local personality to national star on September 27, 1954. Allen's spontaneous, free-form program was an exciting prospect in those first days of television. He said, "While I am frequently introduced on television as 'father of the talk show,' 'as a talk show host the granddaddy of them all,' etc., it was actually Jack Paar who set such programs irrevocably in their present mold.

"[My program] was far more an experimental TV laboratory. One night, for example, we might book the Count Basie Band and do ninety minutes of music. The next night our show might be structured in the form of a debate between teams of political opponents; on another occasion we might present a thirty-minute dramatic show within the context of the ninety-minute form.

"Our production team during those first three years in fact was so experimental, so creative, so innovative that it is literally the case that absolutely nothing has been done on subsequent talk shows—network or syndicated—that was not originally introduced during that first three-year period. Some of today's hosts, for example, like to take a hand mike, like to wander out into the studio audience and interview people."

Allen takes issue with claims that this kind of innovation was generated by NBC and not himself and his own production staff. Some have erroneously given credit for "creating" *Tonight!* to Pat Weaver. Allen explained that that isn't the case. "Pat and I have long constituted a mutual-admiration society," Allen said. "He was kind enough not only to put me on his network for ninety minutes a night for five nights a week but at a later stage to ask me to do a far more important primetime weekly comedy series. For my own part, I've always thought that Pat was one of the best programming executives in television history.

"It needs to be settled, once and for all, that he had nothing whatever to do with 'creating' *Tonight!*. The program, as I've described it here, had already been created—with no input from the NBC programming people—over a year before Pat and his assistant Mort Werner, had the wisdom to add it to the late-night schedule. The only change that was made was that it was no longer called *The Steve Allen Show* but became known as *Tonight!* because the network had initiated its still-successful morning experiment called *Today*."

Allen's style on *Tonight!* would most certainly set the broadcasting tone for the future. "The Late Show Pitchman and The Question Man are two comedy routines from the 1950s which will look familiar to viewers of one of the present shows," Allen explained. "Even the strange cry 'Whoa-oh,' which mysteriously greets all talk show hosts as they appear on camera at the beginning of a telecast, was originated by trombonist Frank Rosellino on my show a good many years ago. On one of the present programs members of the audience are invited to try to stump the band, by thinking of old or outlandish songs that the orchestra might not know. That, too, comes from the original NBC series."

It was the comedy, however, that was Steve Allen's centerpiece on *Tonight!*. His stable of comedy players would later read like a Who's Who of comedy legends, which included Don Knotts, Louis Nye, and Tom Poston. It was Allen, too, who first brought exposure to two up-and-coming vocalists, Steve Lawrence and Eydie Gorme, who also developed a talent for light comedy. Allen would joke that he discovered the singing couple in the backseat of a car. When Allen needed to fill some space, he would play piano backed up by Skitch Henderson's band and Lawrence and Gorme would sing. Gene Rayburn, who would later gain fame as a game show host in the '70s, served as Allen's on-air announcer.

Allen also had a group of regulars who were not professional players, but were "average Joes," and they were as popular as the pros. One of these regular average citizens, Professor Voss, was a hefty man in his sixties with a German accent.

Professor Voss made one of his visits to *Tonight!* half-naked in a vat of ice water. "Tell me, Professor, to what do you attribute your remarkable physical condition?" Allen asked the man in the vat.

"Well, it's water that does it. You've got to start off each day by drinking plenty of water," was the answer.

"Do you do that?" Allen inquired.

"Oh, yes, indeed. The first thing you must do when you get up in the morning is drink four quarts of water!" Voss replied.

"Wow, four quarts. That's a lot of water. And what do you do then?" Allen queried.

"Well," the professor said evenly, "you stand about three feet from the toilet—" That's as far as Professor Voss got before the audience began roaring in laughter.

It wasn't just with his regulars that Allen scored. One of his sketches was to dress in a police uniform and stop cars outside the theater, with the cameraman following. The bright lights of the theater hid the camera from the traffic; they never knew they were watched by millions of Americans until the next morning.

During one of these episodes, Allen flagged down a taxi. "Where to, chief?" asked the cabbie.

"Just take this to Grand Central, and hurry," Allen said, opening the door and throwing a huge salami into the backseat. The cabbie sped off into the night without another word.

Each bit, each sketch, each episode with an "ordinary citizen" was a piece of contemporary Americana set against the exciting background of the Big Apple seen by millions of Americans as it happened. Steve Allen's wit and charm brought even the most outlandish character on the show just a little closer to the viewers. It was in this way that Steve Allen created the feeling of the original "national living room."

Putting on *Tonight!* wasn't all fun and laughs for Steve Allen. He had his share of minor headaches. "Pat and his associates did indeed attempt to make some minor changes in the program, each of which left those of us who were actually creating it night-by-night open-mouthed with astonishment for the reason that the recommended revisions were uniformly—well, I'm afraid dumb is the most accurate word. Weaver, it bears repeating, was a gifted network programmer but that profession has no necessary connection at all with the actual creating and productions of programs. A network programming executive simply decides which programs he will carry and secondly where they will be placed in his schedule," Allen recalled.

He continued, "To deal with specifics, the first change the NBC people recommended was a nightly report on skiing conditions around the country! When our producer Bill Harbach first told me about this, I laughed heartily, as if he had just said, 'The fellas think we should have a segment every night where we tell people how to cast voodoo spells,' or "They think it would be a very good idea to have a nightly segment on Buddhist theology.'

"The really funny thing is that the NBC people were absolutely serious. I sent a memo to them in which I said, 'I wonder if you gentlemen have conducted any formal research as to what percentage of the American public is involved with skiing at all, and secondly which subsection of that miniscule group might actually be planning to ski as of a given date.'

"Needless to say, no such thought had been given the matter and, to the credit of the programmers, they came to realize that it was pointless to force us to inform our millions of listeners all over the country that there was light snow at Stowe or poor conditions in Aspen. The segment was, after a very brief period, dropped and forgotten.

"A second suggestion was also completely wrong for *Tonight!*, which emphasized comedy. The network fellows thought we should add a serious drama critic—a friend of Jayne's and mine named Robert Joseph. The idea was that he become a regular member of our on-camera team for the purpose of reviewing all the new plays on Broadway. In explaining why the suggestion was absurd for the show, I pointed out (a) a tiny fraction of one percent of our audience would be interested, (b) most of them would live and die without ever having seen a Broadway production, and (c) most plays were failures with unknown actors in leading roles.

"I added that, even in the case of those all-too-rare magical Broadway nights when a truly distinguished drama or great musical opened, almost none of our listeners would know—on the show's opening night—that it was to be recognized as important, and that, if they did want to hear anything about the event, their interests could easily be satisfied by our having the stars appear as guests, doing a number from the musical or something of that sort. Furthermore, Mr. Joseph, although a dear fellow and a perfectly competent critic, was not exactly a walking bundle of charisma, so that even if some such regular segment could have been justified, he was hardly the ideal casting for the assignment.

"This idea, too, was fortunately tossed overboard after a short time."

In the first formative years of television, Steve Allen had become a major personality in the relatively short span of three years, so much so in fact, that NBC handed Allen a weekly comedy-variety program on Sunday evenings at eight. Skitch Henderson said, "He took on the aura of a star within a few months." Allen was head-to-head against the entertainment juggernaut of Ed Sullivan. Although he never gained a real ratings superiority over Sullivan, *The Steve Allen Show* did well, earning a Peabody

Award in 1960, its last year. That program is rerun today on the Comedy Central cable channel.

Allen went on to a weekly comedy hour for ABC and a short-lived return to late-night in 1963. He hosted three seasons of *I've Got a Secret*. Over the years, Allen has written dozens of books, both novels and non-fiction. He stayed in television, and hosted the Emmy Awards program on NBC in 1981.

Aside from *Tonight!*, Allen's best-known television project has been the *Meeting of Minds* series on PBS, which was called "the ultimate talk show," during which he interviewed personalities from history, including da Vinci, Plato, and Attila the Hun. Transcripts of the shows have been published in book form and the actual proceedings are still sold as audiotapes. Allen was inducted into the Television Hall of Fame in 1986.

Yet with this success, some pundits and critics argue that Allen should never have left *Tonight!*, that that program was his pinnacle and everything else was a step down, even if they commanded more attention and larger salaries. Skitch Henderson once recalled that he never saw Steve Allen happier than at the party celebrating his departure from *Tonight!*. Responding to such criticism that had he played his cards right and stayed, he would have been a much bigger success, Allen once said, "In my own case the procession from late night to primetime was a matter of logical consequence, but in Carson's case, he aspires to nothing higher than his present eminence."

For all his ups-and-downs in the past four decades, Steve Allen looks back fondly on those three captivating years exploring the frontier of live television entertainment. He said, "As you may gather, my *Tonight!* show years were happy years. It was tremendous fun to sit there night after night reading questions from the audience and trying to think up funny answers to them; reading angry letters to the editor, introducing the greats of comedy, jazz, Broadway, and Hollywood; welcoming new comedians like Shelley Berman, Jonathan Winters, Mort Sahl, and Don Adams; or singers like the petite Portuguese Rosaria or the gamin-like French girl Genevieve.

"There isn't room here to mention the names of the hundreds of performers who appeared on the show but I would like to express my gratitude for their contributions toward the program's success. My decision to drop it was entirely my own, caused by nothing more mysterious than my being unable, after the first few months, to continue with both the *Tonight!* show and my weekly primetime comedy program. The Sunday evening show had both an audience and a salary many times larger than *Tonight!*'s and so the decision was a simple one.

"The *Tonight!* show was never really hard work. Since it was largely ad-libbed, there was no rehearsal problem. I did become exhausted the summer in Hollywood that I filmed *The Benny Goodman Story* all day and then hurried to the TV studio at night, but the show itself was a constant picnic."

America After Dark: A Late-Night Wasteland

By the time Steve Allen gave up the entire *Tonight!* program, he had already given up the Monday and Tuesday shifts of the show. Two talented individuals had replaced him, Jack Paar and the late Ernie Kovacs. Kovacs had been an extremely adept silly comedian, earning the adjective "zany." He said his silly zaniness began as a boy. "It started when I pretended I was frying the cat in the oven," Kovacs once reported. "I ran into the living room where Mother and Dad were entertaining an old friend—an ex-con who was hiding out from the law and had to do all his visiting at night—yelling, 'Cheddar is on fire! He's in the oven!'

"Mother, Dad, and the ex-con raced into the kitchen. Dad opened the oven, and there was a cardboard cutout of a cat, with a little sign around his neck, saying, 'Phew, that was a close one.'" He later brought this innate outrageousness to the nighttime airwaves replacing Allen. When Allen left for good, he suggested either Kovacs or Paar succeed him as King of Midnight on NBC.

Unfortunately, during '56 and '57, visionary executive Pat Weaver was in the midst of office politics and was on his way out. Apparently, *Tonight!* had been faltering with the sponsors toward the end, and the network's parent corporation, RCA, was eager to axe the show along with Weaver. Kovacs and Paar were out of the picture as NBC premiered *America After Dark* only three days after Steve Allen's final departure.

America After Dark was supposed to be closer to the "light news" element NBC wanted from *Tonight!* that Allen never gave in to. *America After Dark* featured host Jack Lescoulie in New York getting various well-known newspaper columnists—Bob Considine, Vernon Scott, Earl Wilson, and Irv Kupcinet to name a few—to do features on American nightlife. The show bombed immediately, and *America After Dark* became *America in the Dark* as far as American television viewers were concerned. The producer was canned the day after the premiere. "I came to work that day and his office had been cleared out," his secretary said. "He was gone."

"*America After Dark* was so bad viewers went next door to turn it off," said former *Tonight!* writer Walter Kempley.

Newspaper columnists made lousy TV personalities, and the *America After Dark* ship sunk in about six months. Before it went down, NBC tried nearly every gimmick to keep it afloat, including loosely stealing features from Steve Allen's *Tonight!*, most notably including the band and the casual conversation Allen had made an art.

With the defunct hulk of *America After Dark* at the bottom of the ratings, NBC and parent RCA wanted to regain late-night supremacy. Earl Wilson from *America After Dark* clued in an up-and-coming television personality named Jack Paar that NBC was willing to try *Tonight!* again, and that the network was looking to Paar as a potential host.

By this time in 1957, Pat Weaver had left NBC. Before he departed, he made a final recommendation that another young promising personality be found a spot on the network. No one acted on Weaver's advice and the young man named Johnny Carson would wait a few more years to become King of the Night.

5

The Tonight Show Starring Jack Paar

NBC's offer to Jack Paar to host a new *Tonight!* came after a succession of stormy career moves. NBC hired Paar away from a CBS weekday afternoon show. "It was a pleasant show, with Edie Adams, Martha Wright, and Jack Haskell, but...there were so few people watching us it would have been cheaper to phone them," Paar later quipped in his usual fashion.

Again, NBC tried to wrestle creative control away from its new maverick host, but once again the host stuck to his guns and the network relented; after "America in the Dark", NBC had precious little to lose.

The late-night airwaves lit up once more, this time as *The Tonight Show*, on July 29, 1957, and again broadcast live from the Hudson Theatre in the Big Apple. The debut, in the eyes of critics and young host alike, was a "disaster." According to Paar, "On [the debut] show, I grappled with a heavyweight wrestler, threw vegetables at the audience, and fed catnip to a lion. However, none of these incidents were as dangerous as the conversation on the show. The talk was sort of a barroom brawl with the cast using words instead of pool cues and beer mugs. We didn't perform; we just defended ourselves."

People soon took to this new helping of midnight mayhem just as they had to Allen's. Paar explained that "before long we had 154 stations, an estimated 30 million viewers weekly, and so many sponsors I felt guilty when I interrupted the commercials with the program.

"When I took over the show on July 29, 1957, it followed a disaster called *America After Dark* which ranks high, I am told by connoisseurs of such matters, among TV's all-time darkest hours. To my surprise, as much as anyone's, our modest, low budget display of violent informality became a hit."

Paar still wanted to mold the show. For instance, he started out doing sketch comedy of the same sort Steve Allen had done, or that Jerry Lester had done before that. But Paar didn't feel he could carry off characters; he was himself, and that was it, funny or not. When he made that decision, Paar told his writer, "Kid, I've made a decision. No more sketches. From now on, I go on with a monologue about my wife and child. Any laughs I get will be from the first-person singular." The near-legendary nighttime monologue was born.

That decision was influenced by the major focus of the show, conversations Paar held with invited guests—some of those conversations quite serious. Paar felt his credibility in those conversations would be damaged if he appeared as a slapstick artist. He told a *Tonight* writer at the time, "We are going to be destroyed if ten minutes later [after an interview] I am wearing a police suit or a sailor outfit. They are never going to believe both Jack Paars. I am going to stay with the honest one—the Midwest Presbyterian."

The straight, non-sketch character approach by no means restricted Paar's talent. Paar recreated the feeling of the national living room that Allen had begun several years before. Paar's interviews were good parlor conversations, and his monologues provided a certain intimacy; in them, Paar talked about his daughter Randy's first bra and his secretary's engagement. The American viewing audience felt a kinship with the host. Paar's predecessor Steve Allen said it best, later observing, "Jack Paar revealed almost everything about himself. Paar was quite prepared—indeed probably eager—to let viewers know how he felt about either the experiences of his life or matters of the moment on *The Tonight Show*.

"While I am frequently introduced on television as 'father of the talk show,' 'as a talk show host the granddaddy of them all,' etc., it was actually Jack Paar who set such programs irrevocably in their present mold," Allen later clarified. "It was Jack Paar who invented the couch, by which I mean it was Jack who, evidently perceiving that this particular approach was far simpler than coming up with outlandish or creative ideas every night, simply decided to book four amusing guests or interesting guests regularly and leave it all at that."

Paar's guests, however, were more than simply "amusing or interesting"; he interviewed JFK when he was still a senator and Bobby when he was Attorney General. Bob Shanks, Paar's talent coordinator, has long acknowledged the influence that *Tonight Show* appearances had on Jack Kennedy's election to the presidency.

Paar himself was an interesting personality that attracted an audience. Dick Cavett, who once worked as a *Tonight Show* writer, said, "Jack in all his work let his own quirks, neuroses, suspicions and dislikes play freely on the surface, along with his enthusiasms, instant reactions and emotional knee jerks. Even for those who didn't like it, it was compelling, and you had to admit that it appealed, if only to a voyeur instinct.

"There was always the implied possibility in his manner that he would explode one day, and you might miss seeing a live nervous breakdown viewed from the comfort of your own bedroom. No matter who the guest was, in a two-shot your eyes were on Jack."

Paar was completely a character; warm, friendly and palling around with a guest one minute, then ascerbic, biting, and ready to get at important ideas the next. *Time* magazine said that Paar was "all the world's straight man...And yet, Paar can hit. A caustic remark, a misconstrued question, a real or fancied attack in or out of the studio can provoke stinging repartee."

Paar mirrored the feelings of all Americans; he was un-inhibited, and when he buddied up to a guest, the audience seemed to feel close to the guest, as well. Paar would also let a guest have it when necessary, and then the audience thought, "I wish I could have said that."

Jack Gould, then the TV critic from *The New York Times*, put it this way, "Mr. Paar is not the traditional trouper; he is a creation of television. If he began as a light humorist, his forte on his own show has been an outspokenness that has not alienated viewers weary of nice-nellyism and self-appointed sacred cows who can dish out criticism but cannot take it.

"The Fourth Estate would be well advised to take heed and, in this instance, not dismiss Mr. Paar as a buffoon with inadequate references; he is echoing a point of view widely held by responsible and sensible people."

Gould was evidently right, because by Paar's second year, his ratings were higher than those of Steve Allen at his peak.

6

Paar For the Course

The streak of intelligent defiance that Jack Paar displayed throughout his *Tonight Show* career began early in his non-conformist life. He grew up in Jackson, Michigan, his parents of Dutch ancestry. Even in his childhood, he set the establishment on its ear. Young Jack was an exceptionally bright child, and school bored him. "I was born an old man," he said later in life. Boredom led to mischievousness, and Jack often played hooky. His mother understood her son's schooltime ennui and assisted him to the point of writing excuse notes for him. Once, Mrs. Paar wrote the school principal to tell him that Jack couldn't travel to school one day in a snowstorm because her son was snowblind!

Jack spent much of his free time fishing with his father, who was a railroad worker. Jack's early years were marred by tragedy. His older brother died when he was five, and his best friend died five years after that. Jack became a serious young man, his room was kept spotless and he had a sign on the door that read: "Keep Out—This Means You."

Things began to look up for Jack after he recovered from a bout with tuberculosis. He did well in high school, yet continued to play hooky. When a radio reporter stopped Jack on the street one day and Jack expounded on the wrongs of the Michigan prison system, his life was changed forever. That reporter practically had to pry the microphone out of Paar's hand with a crowbar.

Afterward, Paar got a job at the station sweeping and emptying wastebaskets for $3 a week. It wasn't fame or fortune, but it

was a start. He found a mike and installed it in the attic in his home. Into it, he read plays, books, magazines, anything to develop a voice he could use on-air. He hit the airwaves when a station offered him a full-time job at $12 a week.

When he got his cleaning job, Jack's school absenteeism became more pronounced—when he got the $12 a week position, he cut his academic ties completely. "The next morning I went into my teacher and said, 'I want my dollar deposit on my locker back.'" Paar explained years later.

"'Why?' the teacher asked in surprise.

"'I'm quitting school,' I announced.

"The teacher was so startled he handed over the dollar. That ended my formal education. When I got home I told my parents I had quit school to be a full-time radio announcer. My father said, 'Oh?' My mother said, 'Oh, is that right?' That's all there was to it."

Paar quit school and devoted himself to his newfound life's vocation. "The words, 'This is station WIBM, Jackson,' will probably never go ringing down the corridors of time with such deathless phrases as 'I shall return,' 'Hi-yo, Silver,' 'Dr. Livingstone, I presume,' and 'You may fire when ready, Gridley.' Yet to me it will always be one of the most beautiful phrases in the English language," Paar later remarked.

"It was the first phrase I spoke when I became a full-fledged radio announcer at the age of sixteen in Jackson, Michigan. In fact, for a long time it was the *only* phrase they would let me speak.

"They wouldn't let me do commercials because I stuttered, and the station was so small you could walk out of its coverage area by going down the street for a cup of coffee, but I was a real live radio announcer. Gradually, though, I progressed beyond station breaks and emptying wastebaskets. The station began letting me spin records and even do a few commercials."

Paar moved on to WIRE in Indianapolis, but returned to WIBM after six months because of homesickness. "Although I was seventeen, and still had little experience, the fact that I had been 'clean to Indianapolis' impressed my former colleagues in Jackson and they treated me with a new respect," Paar said.

Once on the air, Paar began to stir things up. Paar was to announce the national and world news right after the "Town Crier" delivered the local happenings. The "Town Crier", however, ran way over into Paar's time slot. The young Paar was understandably miffed. "'The Town Crier has taken so much time,' I grumbled into the microphone, 'with his items about Mrs. Howell spraining her ankle, the Reillys' missing fox terrier and next Tuesday's strawberry social at the Methodist church that I won't have time for the news of Mussolini's attack on Ethiopia. Good night.'

"The manager grabbed me as I came out of the studio and fired me." After that, Paar began a nomadic career moving from station to station, but he had already proved he was his own person, not bending to authority.

His wanderings were halted when Paar signed up to enter World War II. "I volunteered for the draft in Buffalo, New York, where I had taken refuge at radio station WBEN after leaving Cleveland where I was fired by the station for poking fun at the way the executives' wives jockeyed for position at the annual station picnic," Paar recalled. He added, "War is hell, as General Sherman said, and World War II made me simply furious. I was assigned to bolster morale and, despite my best efforts, I'm sure there were times when the Army wondered which side I was on."

Paar had gained quite a reputation as an independent-minded comedian for the troops. Journalist Sidney Carroll had heard of Paar and travelled to meet him to do a story on the young entertainer for *Esquire* magazine. When he was discharged, Paar called his mother. He learned that movie studios and radio networks had been trying to reach him since the magazine article broke.

Instead of slogging back to the local radio circuit, Paar went to New York. "I went to New York and appeared on a big national program with Ethel Merman and the response was so warm I broke down and wept on the air," he remembered fondly.

To secure his newfound success, Paar and his new bride, Miriam, moved to Hollywood. "Hollywood was like Guadalcanal with houses," Paar later said, recalling his war days.

He signed with RKO for a whopping $350 a week but rarely saw himself in front of the cameras. "I got a sports car, wore dark glasses, posed for still pictures; I did everything an actor does except act. They used to send me on tours to promote pictures I wasn't even in," Paar quipped.

The hopeful star finally did see himself get to the silver screen in a few pictures. A couple stood out in his mind. Twentieth Century cast him in *Love Nest*, opposite another up-and-coming talent, Marilyn Monroe. "Looking back I guess I should have been excited, but I found her pretty dull. Marilyn spoke in a breathless way which denoted either passion or asthma," Paar later wisecracked. "She was always holding up shooting because she was talking to someone on the phone. Judging from what's happened, though, I guess she had the right number."

Paar was always his own person and never played the Hollywood games. Because of that, he lost what may have sent him into the history books. "While at RKO I played a small part in a picture with an attractive comedienne named Lucille Ball. One day, she and I and the producer, Bob Sparks, were watching some rushes in the projection room. I played a light comedy role in the picture and as we sat in the dark watching it, Miss Ball said: 'Jack, do you know any young actor who does light comedy like you do in this role who would like to play opposite me in a new TV series?'"

Paar rattled off the names of competent acquaintances. "I see," Ball responded. After she left, Sparks chastised, "You dumbbell! Don't you get it? She meant you. Why didn't you suggest yourself?"

"Gosh, I never thought of that," Paar responded truthfully. Lucille Ball tapped her husband Desi Arnaz for the role she offered to Paar, and the two went on to make television history with *I Love Lucy*. Paar's own piece of television history wasn't *too* far behind. He would do it his own way.

7

Paar Takes the Night

Several years went by. Then Paar got his own break without Lucy. NBC hired him to host their resurrected *Tonight Show*. He may not have been the next Jimmy Stewart, but his intelligent wit brought the masses back to midnight television. "Someone once defined a filmed television show where anything can happen, but never does," Paar explained. "Our show, on the other hand, is one of the few freewheeling, live, video-in-the-raw programs where anything can happen and sometimes we wish it wouldn't—at least so often.

"Once, while doing a commercial for Bufferin, I actually had a headache so I decided to take two tablets. I took the top off the bottle but couldn't get out the wad of cotton to get the tablets. Trying ingenuity, I poured a little water into the bottle and took a sip. Then I corked the bottle. Little did I know that the action of the water on the tablets in the capped bottle would have a detonating effect. A few seconds later the bottle exploded, showering me and our guests with enough soggy Bufferin to cure headaches for the whole studio audience."

Despite the antics—planned and unplanned—the secret ingredient for the new *Tonight Show*'s success was people. It was for the personalities, both the guests and Paar himself, that people were tuning in. "I'm a people jockey," Paar explained during his NBC heyday, "and what people!

"The thing that has pleased me most about the success of the show is that it is a triumph of honesty. Whenever I say something and add, 'I kid you not,' I'm not kidding. It's a modest show, of light conversation and pleasant entertainment, but it's live and real and true. When you tune in you may see a star born or a joke die. We don't pretend to be anything we're not. I don't feign surprise when a guest I know is coming up. When Elsa Maxwell or Zsa Zsa Gabor take out after someone my terror is real. When I've wept on the air, as I sometimes have, the tears were real and not applied by the make-up man. And when there is laughter on the show it's real and spontaneous."

Paar wasn't without his troubles and his detractors. His outspoken nature rankled the network executives, including RCA president Robert Sarnoff. Paar, who was always emotional as well as outspoken, had a running feud with *TV Guide*. The magazine had published an untrue story about Paar, and refused to print a retraction. As a result, Paar castigated *TV Guide* owner at the time, Walter Annenberg on the air, telling all the stories that Annenberg had suppressed for years. Sarnoff felt that this altercation over the airwaves was an embarrassment for the network and ordered Paar to stop. Of course, Paar went right ahead bashing Walter Annenberg.

"I've been in hot water so often that instead of an Emmy I've been given a gold thermometer. My midnight utterances seem to have occasioned more uproar than any similar nocturnal outcries since Paul Revere," Paar himself admitted.

Paar got in a little deeper when he scheduled John Crosby as a guest on *The Tonight Show*. Crosby was a television critic at the time who had written negative things about the NBC network. Sarnoff balked and told Paar to cancel Crosby. Paar once more refused, and Crosby appeared, only to have his face washed out electronically over the airwaves. Whether this was coincidence or retribution has remained unclear.

Paar raised the ire of Jimmy Hoffa when he had Bobby Kennedy, then the counsel to the Senate Anti-Rackets Committee, on the show. Kennedy urged the public to support a bill aimed against Hoffa and his cohorts. After that appearance, Hoffa filed a joint lawsuit against Kennedy, Paar, and NBC. According to Paar, he was known as "The Defiant One" at the network. "Speaking honestly has been hazardous ever since Socrates drank the hemlock," Paar warned, "and doing so with several million people watching hasn't reduced the risk noticeably."

Paar reached his final straw when his own material was attacked as being "off color." The material in question was a skit about a "W.C."—water closet—or bathroom, and Paar insists it was not "smutty." "I never approved of off-color stories, on or off the air," Paar explained. "On the show, I have always tried to have our lady guests avoid low-cut gowns and wiggling behinds. I have frequently asked comedians to drop jokes which I considered risque from their routines when they appeared on the program."

The skit itself was very much in a Monty Python vein, and was barely suggestive even by late '50s and early '60s standards. Yet the skit was censored. The next evening, Paar had his revenge planned. His secretary had caught on: "Jack had a way of letting you know something was up."

When he went on, he was ready. "It was nearly midnight. In less than an hour it would be the birthday of Abraham Lincoln—the man who freed the slaves. So I emancipated myself from the program," Paar later said. "I explained to the audience what happened and told them how deeply I felt about the matter. Then I walked out of the studio and turned the program back to the censors. Having been fired a number of times by networks, I finally fired a network."

He walked out. The reaction was strong and immediate. He was splashed over the newspapers the next morning. Paar went to a friend's quiet hotel in Florida to hide out while NBC brought out a line of replacement hosts. NBC executive Robert Kintner finally tracked Paar down and went to see him. Kintner finally persuaded Paar to come back after a cool-down vacation in Hong Kong. Kintner's persuasion must of been strong, because Paar's secretary, Mitzi, said, "He really hadn't intended to come back."

Paar returned to the midnight airwaves about a month after he left. Paar stayed with the show from March, 1960 to March of 1962. Paar was tiring of the politics and the infighting, however. He had a running feud going between *The Tonight Show* and *The Ed Sullivan Show*. According to Paar, it was a feud begun by Sullivan. Either a star could be a guest on *Tonight* or *Sullivan*, but not both. It was a dispute from which Paar saw the unpleasant side of stardom, the fact that many performers got their big breaks on *The Tonight Show* only to abandon Paar for the bigger ratings pond of *Sullivan*. "Others swore eternal gratitude for the break, after exposure on our show had zoomed them to stardom, only to be struck dumb at a time when I could have used their moral support in my hassle with Ed Sullivan," Paar revealed, frankly.

"Myron Cohen, the talented monologist, was another performer who went AWOL when Sullivan served his ultimatum. Not long before, when Cohen had been criticized for telling dialect stories, I defended him on the air, saying that he handled his stories with such good taste that no one could take offense. Cohen sent me a warm telegram expressing his thanks and saying that he was looking forward to appearing on our show in the near future. His appearance was scheduled the night that Sullivan dropped his bombshell and Cohen was the first to cancel."

Like Steve Allen before him, Jack Paar accepted a weekly primetime slot for higher pay. This show did well for a few years, but once it got bumped to ABC, it went downhill fast. The show died in 1973, and soon after Paar retired, resigning from his union. Summing up his career, especially those stellar *Tonight Show* years, Paar said, "You've had your chance and now he's gone."

Like with Allen's *Tonight* years, most copies of Paar's appearances have long since seen dust. Paar tossed his personal copies into his trashcan, only to have his neighborhood garbage collector take them and screen them for his family. Before his retirement, Paar did well financially for himself and his family. It was only about a decade ago that Paar booked passage for himself and Miriam in the most luxurious stateroom aboard the *QE-II*. Although he has had no desire to discuss it, he was also able to lend $30,000 to save a friend's mortgage without any mention of prompt repayment.

Paar remains, however, television's original rebel. He would be a hard act to follow, and Johnny Carson would have to prove himself equal to the task.

8

The Great Carsoni

Like Jack Paar, Johnny Carson brought a solidly Midwestern feel to *The Tonight Show*. Carson was born John William Carson in Corning, Iowa October 23, 1925. His father, Homer "Kit" Carson, was a manager for Iowa and Nebraska Light and Power. Because of that occupation, Kit had to move his family around while Johnny was growing up. The Carsons settled for a time in Avoca, Iowa, of which Johnny's main memory is of when he, at the age of eight, escorted Peggy Leach to the movies.

Young Johnny had to leave Avoca and Peggy behind in the third grade. Kit Carson was promoted and transferred to Norfolk, Nebraska. The family loaded their possessions into a borrowed truck and drove west in 1933. To Johnny, Norfolk, with a population at the time of 10,000, was a huge city. Kit moved his family into a comfortable frame house, surrounded by huge trees. Johnny and his brother Dick shared one bedroom; sister Catherine had her own.

Johnny entered the Grant Elementary School, and like Steve Allen and Jack Paar, was fascinated by radio. The young boy was enraptured by *The Jack Benny Show*. "There comes a time or a moment when you know in which direction you're going to go," Johnny explained many years later. "I know it happened to me when I was quite young. I think it's when you find out that you can get in front of an audience and be in control. I think that happened in grade school, fifth or sixth grade, where I could get attention by being different, by getting up in front of an audience or even a group of kids and calling the attention to my-

self by what I did or said or how I acted. And I said, 'Hey, I like that feeling.'"

As he grew up in Norfolk, his search for attention gave Johnny the reputation of a bully, or as one neighbor called him, "the orneriest kid in the neighborhood." "We were very big on BB guns," remembered his brother Dick. "One Christmas, Johnny and I took our BB guns and shot all the balls off our Christmas tree."

As he got a little older, Johnny was able to channel his extravert tendencies into less dangerous pursuits. At the age of twelve, Johnny got a magic kit. "I spent hours at it," Johnny remembered. "Magic became my all-consuming interest."

He practiced and practiced for hours at a stretch. "He could be a pest," admitted Johnny's mother, Ruth. "He was always going around asking, 'How does this look?' 'Did you see that?' It seemed like he was always at your elbow with a trick."

When he was skilled enough, young Johnny took on a persona for performance. He became "The Great Carsoni," and he also began to pursue the art of ventriloquism. For Christmas, Ruth gave her son a magician's table with which to perform. Johnny was a natural. "Johnny had excellent audience control even at that age," said one high school friend. "He was a darn good magician. Whenever he got a spare dollar, he would buy a new trick."

Johnny's first audiences were in front of his mother's bridge club and church socials. At fourteen, Johnny made his professional debut at a Rotary Club function. He was paid $3. "Then I began to get a fee like that at picnics, county fairs, 4-H clubs, service clubs, chambers of commerce. I was billed as 'The Great Carsoni,' wearing a cape my mother had sewn for me," Carson remembered.

During his thirty years as the host of *The Tonight Show*, Carson was spirited and outgoing on the air, yet intensely private in his personal life. This dichotomy began much earlier, during his school years. "John was kind of a loner," said friend and schoolmate Charles Howser. "He was always funny. He kind of made his own space. He was all by himself even when he was with the guys. You'd have six people in a group walking into school and he'd be by himself. Yet in school he liked to be the center of attention."

Johnny never left behind his mischievous streak. In high school chemistry, he was the "Carbide Kid" because of a mix of potassium carbide and water. He set it over heat and the entire laboratory was filled with smoke. That wasn't his only scientific gag. "He somehow put hydrogen sulfide into the school's ventilating system," said another friend. It made such a stink, school was let out for the day, and Johnny was never caught.

There was more to high school for Carson than chemistry pranks. He tried out for football his senior year. "The first time I ran with the ball and got tackled, the next thing I remember is the coach looking down in my face and asking if I was all right," Carson recalled. "He recommended that I give my full extracurricular time to other activities."

Carson found activities of a sexual nature, and his success was greater than with football. "As in all small towns there are certain 'nice' girls, girls that you marry—and girls you do not," Carson explained. "Well, there was this girl, I'll call her Francine, and Francine, well, put out—at least that's what was going around. I finally got up enough nerve to ask her out, she said yes, and you can imagine my excitement...Mount Vesuvius! But then I had to overcome a problem—protection. I went up to the drugstore counter and the druggist yells, 'Well, John, what can I do for you?' Luckily then he saw that I had Francine waiting outside in the car and he knowingly handed over the goods. I remember I had, as we used to put it, a 'swell' time."

As graduation approached, The Great Carsoni put on his last boyhood performance at the school awards assembly. One teacher told him, "You will go far in the entertainment world."

9

Midnight Star from Nebraska

After graduation, Carson entered the Navy. World War II was in full swing, and back in Norfolk, Carson had taken the lead in the local war effort by organizing the town's scrap metal drive. Rather than go overseas to battle, most of Carson's military career was confined to engineering training at Milsaps College. Carson was stationed in Guam after the war had ended. Through it all, he used his skills as a magician, ventriloquist, and comedian to entertain the troops. Like Paar, Carson frequently took comedic aim at the officers to lighten the mood.

After leaving the service, he finished his college education. He wasn't very popular; many classmates mistook a quick wit and a desire for privacy as an air of superiority. "Johnny was quick as a trigger with his mouth," remembered one classmate. "He had a kind of superior air. He didn't want to be involved in any of the rough stuff. He disappeared during Rush Week. It still bugs me, and I don't watch *The Tonight Show*."

Carson had more than his share of opportunities to hone his performance skill. His crowning moment came as emcee of the fraternity talent show. Carson appeared before 5,000 and performed his material between the other skits. He filled his act with sex jokes, the kind which appear daring while remaining tasteful that would become so famous later on *The Tonight Show*.

He graduated with a degree in radio and speech and went to work for radio station WOW. Merle Workhoven, an announcer for WOW, had seen one of Carson's college shows and was very

impressed. Workhoven pushed WOW's program director to get Carson a job. The director replied, "Oh, yeah, we already know about him. It's all in the bag. We've already made a commitment to hire him as soon as he graduates."

At WOW in Omaha, Johnny Carson had a forty-five minute show during which he played records, read the news, sports, and weather, and engaged in the banter which would make him famous. Carson's show was broadcast as far away as South Dakota, Iowa, and Missouri. His radio training was very much like that of both Steve Allen and Jack Paar, and all three would be a sort of "disc jockey of television" on *The Tonight Show*.

Now earning $47.50 a week, Carson decided he could marry his magician's assistant and college sweetheart, Jody Wolcott. "I expected John to be the boss," Jody Carson later explained. "There wasn't any equality in our marriage, but I didn't expect there to be. It was all John wanted."

Carson was there when mighty WOW went to television broadcasting. WOW-TV began by broadcasting a test pattern, and all over, people would find TV sets to stare at this pattern. In Nebraska, as in most places, especially the isolated ones, television was a phenomenon. "Television is being singled out for its virtues," the local Omaha newspaper editorialized. "One of them is a curb on juvenile delinquency. In Scarsdale, New York, for example, juvenile delinquency sank nearly to zero as ownership of television receivers rose."

When actual broadcasting began, programming was meager in Nebraska; it was difficult to get the network that far out of New York. Carson was given his own show at 12:30 p.m. each day for fifteen minutes. He called his program *Squirrel's Nest*. "The trick was just finding something to do," Carson explained. "We had turtle races, one of the more exciting things."

He became a celebrity, between WOW and his magic shows, for which he then charged a princely $25 per performance. But Carson wanted to succeed, and Nebraska was known more for wheat than celebrities. Carson, his bride Jody, and their new-born son Chris moved West to San Francisco in his beaten up Oldsmobile and a U-Haul trailer. San Francisco turned up dry for Carson, and they moved further south to Los Angeles.

In L.A., Carson met up with Bill Brennan, a friend from way back in Avoca, Iowa. Brennan was employed at station KNXT-TV. Brennan eventually got Carson a position as an announcer. Where Carson had been a big television fish in the small pond of Omaha, he now became the guppie who worked menial chores and the New Year's shift. "I remember those first months in Hollywood when we used to look out over the hills, in the Toluca Lake area," Johnny recalled. "And I remember saying, 'Bob Hope lives right over there.'"

His on-air talent was soon recognized, and the real climb to fame began when his show, *Carson's Cellar,* made its debut—it was a bargain-basement spoof, but it helped him sharpen his in-character skits and on-air conversational style. He made an extra $50 for the program, but had to maintain his regular announcing duties.

Carson's Cellar wasn't the pinnacle of the station's line-up, but it did eventually catch the eye of a CBS executive. *Carson's Cellar* became the classier *The Johnny Carson Show*, broadcast regionally in the West. In its more urbane format, it was mediocre, and fizzled. It tried to make a comeback to no avail. "There were too many cooks telling me what to do and how to do it," Carson explained. "There was no central control. The agency was putting people on without telling me. I was sitting around like a dummy." It was a mistake he wouldn't make again.

Carson did some comedy writing, most notably for Red Skelton, and, ironically, sat in occasionally for Jack Paar while Paar was still the host of CBS' morning program. Carson jumped at the offer to host his own program, a daytime game show, *Do You Trust Your Wife?*. It was a step down from his own variety show, especially because it was broadcast on last-place ABC. But it was an on-air job, and Carson relocated himself and his family to New York, from where the show was broadcast live. Jody had given birth to their third son, Cory, by then. Pressures had strained the marriage between Johnny and Jody, especially the financial uncertainty while raising three children. Jody hoped New York would improve their lives.

When Carson joined, the show became *Who Do You Trust?* to allow unmarried contestants. While the spontaneous appearance of *Who Do You Trust?* looked as if it would make a good training ground for the improvisation of *The Tonight Show*, even Carson's ad-libs were included in the script. *Who Do You Trust?* was yet another forum for his almost-risque sexual banter.

After a time on the gameshow, Carson had to fill the announcer's position on the program. He interviewed Philadelphia personality, Ed McMahon. "Nobody's ever going to make me believe that jive about thirteen being unlucky," McMahon later revealed, after getting the job. "It was October 13, 1958, that Johnny and I started together on *Who Do You Trust?*."

It was the beginnings of one of television's most memorable, and long-lasting, partnerships. "I was just the announcer," McMahon explained, "the guy who opened the show, read the commercials, and brought out the questions that Johnny asked the contestants. Pretty soon he began making remarks about my size. 'Here comes Big Ed.' Then he started that bit of mythology about my drinking. To defend myself, I'd drop in a zinger every once in a while. Gradually our relationship, both professional and personal, began to develop."

Carson and his sidekick McMahon remained on *Who Do You Trust?* for four years, although in an interesting twist of fate, he was called upon to substitute once more for Jack Paar. This time it was 1958, and he became guest host of Paar's *Tonight Show*. Carson was baptized in late-night by Groucho Marx.

When, in March, 1960, it appeared Jack Paar had walked off *The Tonight Show* for good, Carson's agent, Al Bruno, began trying to convince Carson to take the opening. Carson was wary;

Paar was a television heavyweight; Carson reasoned that following such a dynamic personality would spell career disaster. Paar returned to his program, and the question seemed moot, except to Al Bruno, who saw the eventuality of Paar's final departure. Bruno kept at Carson.

10

Prince Johnny Takes the Reigns

"There are not too many communicators in this business, and I certainly thought he was one," said Al Bruno, remarking about Johnny Carson. "At no point did I feel that I was mistaken in this view, and I felt he certainly had the talent."

Carson's popularity as the amiable host of *Who Do You Trust?* had done wonders for ABC's pathetic ratings. This fact was not lost on rival NBC. When Paar finally gave up *The Tonight Show* in '62, Bruno practically worked overtime to convince Carson to offer himself for the job. Carson evidently toyed with the idea, mentioning it to industry friends. One friend, comedian Tom Poston, had gotten his jumpstart to stardom as one of the company of funnies on Steve Allen's original *Tonight!*.

Poston wasn't enthusiastic. "Nobody can follow Jack," Poston warned Carson. "You've got to let somebody else take it. He'll bomb. Then you'll come in. You'll be compared to the bomber, and not the king of the night."

Carson was Mort Werner's choice to succeed Paar. Werner was Pat Weaver's successor at NBC programming, and apparently, almost as visionary. Evidently, Werner put his career on the line with his advocacy; Carson couldn't take over the host's position for six months after Paar's departure because he was bound contractually to *Who Do You Trust?*. In those six months without a stable host, *The Tonight Show* could've run out of steam. It almost did; by the time Johnny took the helm on October 1, 1962, most of the program's advertisers had bailed out. Carson had to be *very* good to keep the program alive.

Paar's last night on *The Tonight Show* was March 30, 1962; it was an intimidating act to follow. Several celebrities came to bid tribute and goodbyes to TV's most-talked-about personality. Stars served as ballbearers, carrying Paar on stage in a coffin. When the program was broadcast next, it began a long, six-month succession of fill-in hosts. Everyone from Groucho Marx to Soupy Sales to Hugh Downs tried their hand. It was well-known that Carson was a shoe-in, so the substitutes weren't very enthusiastic.

A few minutes before Carson's debut, Skitch Henderson, the *Tonight* bandleader, wished the new star good luck. Henderson was an old *Tonight* hand, having been with the program since Steve Allen's debut almost a decade earlier. Carson didn't say anything in reply, but Henderson later said he could see the look of pure terror in Carson's eyes.

NBC made the most of the debut of the new *Tonight Show*—the guest list was impressive, including Joan Crawford, Rudy Vallee, Tony Bennett, and Mel Brooks. Carson was anything but confident. On that opening night, Carson suggested, "Jack Paar was the king of late-night television. Why don't you just consider me the prince?"

Despite his anxiety, his opening night earned good notices from TV critics. In his column the next day, Jack Gould commented, "Mr. Carson's style is his own....He has the proverbial engaging smile and the quick mind essential to sustaining and seasoning a marathon of banter.

"At the outset he said he was not going to describe every guest as an old and dear friend, an indication of a refreshing attitude against prevalent show-business hokum. A healthy independence without overtones of neuroses could wear very well."

Who Do You Trust? had been heavily scripted, each moment carefully planned. Compared to that, *The Tonight Show* was utter, ad-libbed chaos. But Carson had improvised before; all he needed was practice. He felt more comfortable, however, having brought his sidekick, announcer McMahon. The two travelled together to the pre-premiere planning sessions in Florida. "Comes October 1, 1962, sitting around a table in Fort Lauderdale, Florida, and the producer, the director, the writers, the star, are all trying to figure out exactly what kind of show the Carson version of *The Tonight Show* would be," McMahon recalled.

He continued, "I was there only because I was half of the regular cast, but I didn't have anything to say about what the format should be. I did, however, enjoy being in Florida because there always came when the conference tables turned into golden coaches and we went to the ball.

"On the plane back to New York I said to Johnny, 'How do you see my role in this show? What's my stance? How do I fit in? What function do you envision me as performing?'

"He said, 'Ed, if you mean, what are you going to do, let me put it to you this way. I don't even know what I'm going to do. So let's just play it by ear and see what happens.' We've been doing that ever since."

Carson's early days were haphazard and unplanned, and at the same time, over-planned, without room for spontaneity. When a guest was a bore and bombing, taking the program with them, Carson had no room to cut away. If an interview was fifteen minutes, he had to stick with it, even if each moment was agony for the audience as well as him. Conversely, if one guest proved extremely successful and was wowwing Carson and crowd, after his or her fifteen or twenty minutes, they were gone.

To his credit, Carson knew that if he wanted staying power, he needed to pace himself. He couldn't come out night after night with material that took six months to work up because eventually he couldn't top himself and he and the audience would burn out. His formula worked. In his early months, Carson was scoring a 21 rating, or 58 percent of the nighttime viewing public. Seven and a half million people were tuning in to catch a glimpse at the "new Jack Paar." The "original" Paar, by comparison, would score in the high teens when he was particularly controversial and talked-about.

Carson knew most of his audience wasn't from the West Side of Manhattan, but back in places like Avoca, Iowa; Norfolk, Nebraska; and beyond. "You have to tailor your material to the medium," Carson explained. "I can look fairly well at a piece of material and know fairly well whether it will play and be amusing. You experiment sometimes. I'm sure Mel Brooks is not a comic who reaches the great percentage of the audience. He's kind of wild—but when he's good, he's near genius. I'll put him on the show. I'm much safer with a Sam Levenson. He talks about kids and schools, and he won't offend. You just have to rely on your own judgement. If you do make a mistake, you'll find out soon enough—because suddenly you won't have an audience."

The Tonight Show took on Carson's personality—affable, humorous, and lightly entertaining. Soon after Carson's debut on *Tonight*, his mother said, "I wasn't sure John was the type for it. When Jack Paar had the show, it was more like an arena—so much controversy, all the time. John is a gentle, kind person. He's not controversial. But now I think he'll do all right."

Shelly Schultz, a former *Tonight* talent coordinator, observed, "I think that he is one of those rare phenomenal people who understood the medium. In a very unintellectual way he understood it for what it was. He settled in and played the game every night, and he became very likable. He wasn't one of those who overintellectualize the communications medium and had the danger of failing because you think too much."

Carson lived and worked by his instincts. He had the knack, when he made fun of a group of people—old people with his Aunt Blabby skits, conservatives or liberals with his political jokes—he was able to make a joke while not making an attack. Usually, the people Carson was lampooning were also the ones laughing the loudest. Carson, like his predecessors, had the gift of gab.

Advertisers and viewers ate it up, and soon *The Tonight Show* was grossing several million dollars. Carson was a bargain at $100,000 a year, and was quickly signed for a second year. Despite the success, Carson had problems, both on the show and off.

Overcoming Problems, Despite Success

Johnny Carson may not have thought too much, but he did have other excesses. Alcohol was the most pronounced. It began back on *Who Do You Trust?*. "On Fridays we used to do two shows, a live one at three-thirty in the afternoon, and at seven we taped a show for the following Monday," said Ed McMahon, recalling his pre-*Tonight* days with Carson. "This gave everyone a three-day-weekend. Between those two shows Johnny and I got into the habit of strolling next door to Sardi's little bar for a couple of relaxers which we felt we needed before doing the second show. We only had two hours. How much can you drink in two hours, especially if you're talking business?

"The trouble was that Johnny, as he's said many times on the air, isn't the world's greatest drinking man. Give him three shots and he gets very frisky. And sometimes when we'd come back to tape the Monday show, tongues got tangled and things got said that had to be bleeped." He was to become one of the notorious celebrity drinkers, his drunken escapades grist for the tabloid mill. About twenty years later, Carson discussed his bout with booze on CBS' *Sixty Minutes*, proudly announcing he was firmly on the wagon.

Another ongoing personal problem for Carson was his love life. His marriage to Jody Wolcott Carson having fallen apart, the couple had separated in 1959 during Carson's gameshow stint. The marriage had undergone too much strain all at once from Johnny's career, children, financial struggles, as well as Johnny's drinking and Jody's depression. "Basically, what went wrong was we had three children right away—-the diaphragm was all they had in those days—and there was no money. It happens all the time to a lot of people," the former Mrs. Carson revealed.

After the separation, Johnny began not only to be known as a drinker, but a womanizing drinker. Ed McMahon's manager recalled, "One night Johnny, Ed, and I were at a place on the West Side that was a Mafia hangout. Johnny had quite a bit to drink and he was really weaving. And he saw this attractive blonde. He went over to her and tried to pick her up. Well, this blonde was one of the girls of this top Mafia guy. And the owner of the place got hold of Johnny and took him outside, because the guy would have killed him. Absolutely. And Johnny resisted. He didn't want to go."

Carson is well-known for his intense—almost obsessive—privacy, but one journalist described him as "a loner who was not comfortable being alone, a trait that was almost as effective at driving him to the altar as a shotgun would have been."

This "driving trait" set Carson on the path of courtship of Joanne Copeland. She, too, was in the gameshow industry. When Carson met her, Copeland was Jack Narz's assistant on *Video Village*, an obscure nighttime gameshow in the early '60s. Carson and Copeland began to pursue each other intensively. Copeland's parents had divorced when she was still an infant, and she dreamed of finding the perfect romance for herself. She believed she had found it in Johnny Carson. The two moved in together, and Copeland devoted herself to Carson, going so far as to prepare the food for his weekly poker games.

Yet not all was bliss. "There were a lot of arguments," Jack Narz recalled. "We would double date. The four of us would be out in the country somewhere on his boat. He would get so pissed off at her that we'd get back onshore and he would take her to the train station and get her the hell back to New York." The courtship continued. Carson and his wife Jody had separated, but never officially divorced. Carson finally arranged a true divorce to pave the way for marriage to Joanne. His managers wanted to minimize the scandal that a divorce would cause in the early '60s, so they arranged for Jody Carson to fly to Mexico to obtain the divorce. With the split finalized, Carson married his new bride in August, 1963 while enjoying the success *The Tonight Show* had brought him.

Not all of his problems were of a personal nature. Despite its amazing success, there was something wrong w*The Tonight Show*. It had taken on its new host's quiet, friendly personality, but there wasn't any definition; Carson was locked into a set number of minutes with horribly boring guests.

Art Stark had been Carson's producer on *Who Do You Trust?*, and it had been Stark's ability as well as Carson's talent which took a show teetering on the brink of cancellation and turned it into ABC's ratings centerpiece. Stark moved over to *The Tonight Show* after the NBC staff producer left. He had produced USO shows in World War II, where timing and pacing were key to hold an audience, and he brought that talent to *Tonight*, where it was equally crucial to holding a viewer's interest through ninety minutes.

Stark worked with Carson on the opening monologue, which focused on news and politics. He wanted Carson to avoid caustic commentary, but offer enough bite to give the show excitement. Stark wasn't at all pleased with *Tonight*'s guests. He had the staff get tougher—guests had to have something to *say*. Stark gave Carson more latitude with boring guests. If a guest were dying, they were gone before the viewer at home had the chance to yawn.

"There's no experience I can describe to you that would compare with doin' *The Tonight Show* when he's on it," said one terrified celebrity guest after Stark had taken over. "It is so wired, and so hyped, and so up. It's like Broadway on opening night. There's nothing casual about it. And it's not a talk show. It's some other kind of show. I mean, he has such energy, you got like six minutes to do your thing . . . and you better be good. Or they'll go to the commercial after two minutes. . . ."

Conversely, if a guest caught Carson's interest, there was no hurry to get him or her off the set to put on the next one in line. If a scheduled guest didn't appear after time ran out, Carson made a simple apology and the show would try to reschedule. Stark was a despot, but he wanted unconditional success. He wanted the show to have tempo, rhythm. His format settled into a fifteen minute monologue, comedy sketches, stunts in which Carson participated, such as pitching a baseball with the pros or flying with the Thunderbird stunt air squadron, and, of course, conversations with celebrity and non-celebrity guests.

"It's a chess game," Carson once said of *The Tonight Show*. It was true. For instance, in Carson's earliest months, the show began not at 11:30 which it does today, but at 11:15, after NBC's news. Eventually, the local affiliates began taking the 11:15 to 11:30 slot for their own use. NBC didn't adjust, *The Tonight Show* still began at a quarter past eleven, and many viewers were deprived of Carson's monologue.

That stuck badly in the host's craw. In a move reminiscent of Jack Paar, Carson began to boycott the first fifteen minutes, and McMahon opened the show. That the star was skipping out did not sit well at all with NBC executives, and a skirmish developed between Carson and the top brass—the first of many over the years. NBC relented and *The Tonight Show* moved its opening to 11:30, which paved the way for the format of the thirty-minute local eleven o'clock news broadcast.

12

The Rocky Road to Legend

By the late 1960s, Johnny Carson was off and running as an entertainment dynamo. The ratings for *The Tonight Show* were continuing a steady ascent, and Carson was sought after as a nightclub performer in Las Vegas. In his live club act, he offered the kinds of skits he had done on *Squirrel's Nest* and *Carson's Cellar* years earlier, especially lampoons of television and TV commercials. Carson, who was generally bursting with sexual banter and innuendo on *Tonight*, became risque in his solo act. He broke Judy Garland's attendance record at the Congo Room of the Sahara Hotel. On the other hand, *Looking for Love*, Carson's first attempt at film acting, bombed badly.

The Tonight Show eclipsed Carson's solo fame. It was Carson on *Tonight* that had both viewers and stars buzzing. Mariette Hartley called the experience of being a guest on the show "sexy and exciting." Another of the hottest actresses of the time, Suzanne Pleshette of the sitcom *The Bob Newhart Show*, concurred, calling her appearances "thrilling." The key was Carson's ability to keep his guests on their toes, with the audience never knowing quite what to expect. Kenneth Tynan, a respected drama critic, was an early guest of the program; he expected to be questioned about a talked-about play by Winston Churchill. Tynan recalled, "Carson froze my marrow by suddenly asking my opinion not of Churchill, but of General de Gaulle, and . . . from that moment on, fear robbed me of saliva, so that my lips clove to my gums, rendering coherent speech impossible."

The Tonight Show had become a young comedian's heaven. If an up-and-coming comedian appeared on the show and Carson asked him or her back, that comedian had "made it." A journalist stated, "Unlike Paar, Johnny didn't fancy himself the discoverer and nurturer of young talent. But if you were good, if you made Johnny laugh, then you got invited back, and maybe next time you got to sit down next to Johnny after your bit."

Bill Cosby, Woody Allen, and the late Redd Foxx all began this way. But no one would become more famous—and later infamous— for her *Tonight* beginnings than Joan Rivers. She had been playing small dirty clubs in Greenwich Village before she finally landed on *Tonight* in '65. The second-to-last guest of the night, she wore a black dress, a string of pearls, and a pink boa.

"He wanted it to work," Rivers later stated of Carson at that first performance. "He knew how to go with me and feed me and knew how to wait . . . . He never cut off a punch line, and when it came, he broke up. It was like telling it to your father—and your father is laughing, leaning back and laughing, and you know he is going to laugh at the next one. And he did and he did and he did . . . . At the end of the show he was wiping his eyes. He said, right on the air, 'God, you're funny. You're going to be a star.'"

Rivers came back two weeks later as the first guest, and would become a *Tonight* standard over the next twenty years, eventually becoming Carson's exclusive substitute guest host. The climax of her involvement would shake the very establishment that *The Tonight Show* would become.

That he was developing young struggling talent like Rivers on the program, that he *was* seen as a "father figure," meant Carson was no longer a young struggling talent himself. He had become established, starting down the road to becoming a fixture of contemporary American culture. That sort of tenure brought more viewers, which brought more advertisers, and in the end, more money for the network.

Carson's yearly contracts were renewed quickly and enthusiastically by NBC. Carson knew his worth, and negotiated up in salary with each one. By 1966, he was making a few thousand short of $400,000 a year. Carson was also able to secure more and more control over the show for his personal production company.

Amidst the making of a broadcast legend, *The Tonight Show* was not a band of merry men. Carson and longtime bandleader Skitch Henderson had their continuing problems. This personality clash eventually sent the bandleader from the Allen era into retirement. Trumpeter Carl "Doc" Severinsen came in to fill those shoes. Severinsen had been in t*Tonight Show* band before Carson, and as "sartorial foil," would become as integral to Carson's stage persona as McMahon.

Carson also feuded with sidekick McMahon if he felt McMahon was acting more than second-banana. "Many times I watched Johnny trying to get rid of Ed. It must have been a basic insecurity of some kind on Johnny's part," revealed Henderson. "It really was so silly, because we were all trying to pull the same ship."

Carson was difficult with his workers behind the scenes. He was a perfectionist, demanding nothing less from himself and his staff. More than that, as jovial and affable as he was with his guests and regulars on the air, he was dour and quiet with his staff, unless he was lashing someone for a mistake. As one Carson biographer put it, "Silence was the highest accolade." There was no socializing between Carson and his staff. The one attempt at a dinner party at the Carson residence for *Tonight Show* writers ended with the writers shooting craps in the hallway.

Carson also became dissatisfied with his producer and longtime friend, Art Stark. Bruce Cooper, a former *Tonight* talent coordinator, said at the time, "The first thing he ought to do is fire Art Stark. He's f—-ing up the show so badly . . . and [has] surrounded himself with an army of yes-people." It had been Stark who settled the format of *The Tonight Show* and gave it staying power. Carson wanted to fire Stark, but the producer had two years left on a contract. Carson got some needed ammunition on April 1, 1967 when the television union went out on strike.

Some of Carson's on-air contemporaries, such as NBC news anchorman Chet Huntley, were so infuriated by the strike that they broke through picket lines. Although Carson was never a political or truly controversial personality, he abided by the strike. His wife Joanne felt that her husband had been slighted by the long-term contract he had signed with NBC in '66. She made her feelings known to Carson, who opened negotiations. He was asking for $2 million; NBC wasn't going to pay that.

Carson returned to Nebraska to help commemorate the state's centennial. While he was off the air, NBC broadcast reruns without consulting the host, which enraged Carson. He was particularly piqued because the reruns were from the past Christmas holiday season; the viewing public was watching Carson make winter and Christmas jokes in the middle of Spring. He didn't appreciate that, and demanded that NBC cease the reruns. NBC balked, saying it was within its rights to show the old *Tonight Shows*. Carson issued a statement saying that he was quitting, "effective forthwith." He hoped his threat would force the network to give in to his pay raise.

The union strike lasted only ten days, but Carson didn't return to work, and instructed his staff to do the same. He used his personal strike against Art Stark, issuing a statement saying that if he did return to the show, "there might also be some changes in personnel on the program." None of the other staffers knew that the threat was directly aimed at Stark and the entire production company grew nervous.

Early Challengers

Today, *The Tonight Show* weathers stiff competition each evening from several midnight television challengers, ranging from comedian Arsenio Hall to former President Ronald Reagan's son, Ron Jr. Although each has their own personality, they are all variations on the format Art Stark laid out for *The Tonight Show* thirty years ago.

Until 1967, *Tonight*'s toughest fight was only against thirty-year-old movies. ABC changed all that when they launched *The Joey Bishop Show* in direct competition to Carson's program. Bishop was a popular comedian who had won over audiences only a short time before on *The Tonight Show* as a substitute guest host while Carson was away.

The Joey Bishop threat added stimulus to NBC's resolve. On the evening when Bishop's program debuted, it captured forty percent of the New York ratings. *The Tonight Show*, with Country-Western star Jimmy Dean sitting in for the protesting Carson, made barely a whimper with twelve percent.

Not that Bishop fared well himself. His special guest of the evening, then-Governor of California Ronald Reagan, appeared fifteen minutes late and although Bishop gave guest star Buddy Greco a thunderous introduction, Greco was conspicuously absent when the curtain went up; no one had bothered to cue him and he sat in his dressing room chatting, unaware. After those debacles, *The Joey Bishop Show* only did half as well the next few nights, but still managed to pull ahead of *The Tonight Show* sans Carson.

Carson and NBC renegotiated three days after Bishop premiered; Carson would receive $20,000 a week and $1 million in life insurance. Until then, Carson's private production company paid the salaries of the staff of the show as well as substitute guest hosts. Under the new agreement, NBC picked up the tab, and Carson received payment when NBC broadcast *Tonight Show* reruns. In all, Carson walked away with more than a million dollars. He returned to the show and NBC issued the following statement: "We are delighted at Johnny's return, and we know the feeling is shared by millions of viewers throughout the country who enjoy his unique brand of humor and intimate warmth."

Carson also did away with Stark. Stark had been a petty tyrant from the beginning, but when he first came aboard, that's what the show had needed, structure and discipline. Carson had become more confident in his role on *Tonight* as time went by. On that first Carson *Tonight Show*, he had called Jack Paar the king of midnight, and said he would only be the prince; after winning the million dollar duel with NBC, Carson finally claimed the throne. He no longer wanted the restrictive Stark around.

For weeks, Stark called Carson, asking if his position was secure; each time Carson reassured his old friend that everything was fine. Finally, Carson invited Stark up to his apartment in the United Nations Plaza. There, Carson revealed that he wanted Stark to leave. Carson evidently truly believed that he was doing his friend a great service by delivering the bad news himself, rather than leaving it to the lawyers. Stark stormed out.

In an effort to kill bad publicity over the firing, Carson immediately contacted Gary Stevens, his publicist. The host told Stevens, "You're going to hear that Art Stark has been dropped from the show. I want you to know this so you can fend off these things. And all I can tell you is that Art is a very sick man." Evidence of Carson's clout was that Stark was dropped socially by most everyone, including most *Tonight Show* colleagues. The only two who would continue to have anything to do with him were Joan Rivers and Ed McMahon.

Art Stark was reduced to producing projects like the Junior Miss Pageant. Before Stark, critics and viewers called Carson "plastic," and didn't know the man. After Stark's departure, that changed. The concept Stark created for *Tonight* was not only copied by other late-night competitors, but also found its way into daytime and primetime programming as well. When Stark died in 1982, only McMahon sent a card to his widow.

After King Carson returned to the air, Joey Bishop was no match for *The Tonight Show*. Bishop left the program two years after it began. ABC tried to keep it alive with other hosts, but it soon went under. Dick Cavett became ABC's next midnight contender in '69. Cavett had actually worked as a writer for both Carson and Jack Paar and was no newcomer to late-night. He took a more intellectual approach to the format, scheduling in-depth interviews of the type Paar had done on his *Tonight Show*. Cavett interviewed such personalities as Jack Lemmon, Orson Welles, and Woody Allen. *Time* called it "intelligent alternative programming." Cavett was more cerebral than funnyman Carson, but that proved no advantage. Cavett's show was little more successful than Bishop's, and it went off the air in '73.

None of his rivals had come close to damaging Carson's ratings, but networks kept posing more challenges. CBS sent Merv Griffin into battle against the *Tonight* juggernaut in August, 1969. Griffin, like Carson, was originally a gameshow host, and had hosted daytime talk shows since 1962. British character actor Arthur Treacher served as Griffin's Ed McMahon; it died on the network in '72.

Griffin, however, apparently saw the writing on the wall and had the sense to transfer his program to independent syndication. Although *The Merv Griffin Show* never materialized as a significant threat for *Tonight*, Carson made a habit of poking fun at this particular competitor. It was all in jest, however, as Carson and Griffin have been personal friends. Griffin closed his show and his vast production company, selling off his assets in '86 for hundreds of millions of dollars. It was Griffin who developed the highly popular gameshows *Wheel of Fortune* and *Jeopardy!* Carson and Griffin were also connected because Carson's brother, Dick, served as Griffin's director after Dick Carson left as director of *The Tonight Show*.

None of the late-night opponents proved a serious challenger to *Tonight*'s and Carson's midnight monarchy. The competition did, however, shake the complacency of the *Tonight* team. They couldn't rest on a midnight monopoly, but had to keep seducing their late-night legions.

Tiny Tim and Tonight in Transition

After Art Stark's unceremonious removal, the position of producer was up for grabs. Carson brought in Stan Irwin from Las Vegas at $400,000 a year to produce the show, but Irwin couldn't control the heavy political in-fighting among the staff after the Stark incident.

A man named Rudy Tellez got the job. Tellez had already been with the show as a talent coordinator, one of the staff whose arduous job it is to hunt through all of the vain stars who want the exposure of *The Tonight Show*. They find the few who can meet the demands of Carson-banter, sorting through all the piles of books that authors want to hype, all the cassettes average fans send in of their sons, daughters, brothers, or dogs or cats who they say are the most talented individual in the world and who deserve a spot in America's living room. The talent coordinators plow through all that to choose guests and acts that appeal to viewers.

By the time Tellez became producer, *The Tonight Show* had been stripped of one of its original fascinations; it was no longer a live show at 11:30 from Hudson Theatre in New York City. It was taped earlier in the evening from an NBC studio and broadcast at 11:30 Eastern time.

Even without the pressures of "live" television, Tellez found his job difficult. The battles with Joey Bishop and the other late-night opponents pulled away the veneer of self-satisfaction; *Tonight* needed to hold viewers, and Tellez was experimenting to find the best way to do that. It was a time of transition; the end of

Tonight of the "Golden Age" and the birth of *The Tonight Show* as it has evolved today.

"I would go home some night and say, 'Wait until you see the show tonight. It's incredible. Buddy Hackett dropped his pants and the audience screamed and every guest was better than the last.' I'd turn it on and it wasn't as funny," Tellez recalled. "And some nights I'd come home and say, 'Jesus, don't even watch it. It was a disaster from beginning to end. Johnny was off, the guests were boring.' I'd turn it on, and somehow it went better.

"What television does is take off all highs, take off all the lows, and squeeze them into a little box. That's where *The Tonight Show* shines. It's the bland leading the bland."

Tellez tried a lot of interesting things. He made the show more physical, less abstract, and a little more comic. He continued the idea of Carson doing stunts on the show. Carson had always prided himself on his physique, so Tellez had him jump out of airplanes, all sorts of wild things.

Although Carson's lightened up on the stunts in recent years as he's begun to feel his age, former talent coordinator Craig Tennis said, "Still, in the annals of *The Tonight Show*, there are a host of athletic spots involving Johnny that exist only because I was able to appeal to his physical vanity."

Tellez also revealed what was a frustration with Carson. In the late '60s and early '70s, Carson felt that despite his feature film bomb a decade or so earlier, he could do something beyond *The Tonight Show*. "I think Johnny wanted to be another Jack Lemmon in the worst possible way," Tellez observed. "But he didn't have it. There's a film intensity and a television intensity. On film he doesn't come across as a human being. On television he's this warm person you want to get to know as he sits behind the desk and just talks. On television he capitalizes on that pixie quality of his that enables the audience to say, 'That's a guy I'd like to know. Gee, that's kind of cute.'"

THE STORY OF THE TONIGHT SHOW

Tellez's experimentation with the style of the show to garner higher ratings took some strange turns. None were more strange than the painfully-obvious publicity ploy of the on-air wedding of Tiny Tim to his "Miss Vicki," Victoria Budinger.

Tiny Tim was a true marvel in the late '60s. He wore his hair down to his shoulders and appeared to be one of the hippie set; yet he was as conservative as apple pie without ice cream. He adored women from the ages of sixteen to twenty-five, yet no one knew Tiny's own age. He loved women, but he didn't believe in either sex before marriage or birth control. He began to gain notoriety in clubs in New York not for new rock'n'roll but for singing old tunes and plucking a ukulele. He first appeared on television on Merv Griffin's program, but it is for his *Tonight Show* visits that he is best remembered.

While other guests either sparkled or flopped under Carson's witty banter, Tiny Tim developed a unique relationship with the host. As was talent coordinator procedure, Craig Tennis furnished Carson with background on Tiny Tim in capital letters on Carson's notecards: "TINY TIM IS OUTSPOKEN . . . . HE WILL, AND CAN, TALK ON VIRTUALLY ANY SUBJECT, INCLUDING IMPURITIES IN SOAP. HE IS FOR REAL, BUT WHAT HE *REALLY* IS, IS THE REAL QUESTION."

"Carson felt uncomfortable with me because he didn't know how to react," Tiny Tim later admitted. "I know he felt uncomfortable because of some of my beliefs."

On April 4, 1968, Tiny Tim came out, sang "Tiptoe Through the Tulips," sat down with Carson, and in entertainment writer Albert Goldman's words, "reduced Johnny Carson to his straight man with a few child-like answers." Carson's very persona was based on his ability to turn his guests into *his* straight man; it was that fact that had melted so many guests. With Tiny Tim, the tables were turned, with Carson in the vulnerable position, but Tiny very much respected Carson. "Mr. Carson has the mind of Perry Mason, the real Perry Mason of the books by Erle Stanley Gardner," said Tiny. "In my opinion he's always one step ahead of his guests. His main aim is to win."

As demonstration of *The Tonight's Show*'s power over the audience, Carson hyped Tiny Tim's album *God Bless Tiny Tim* and the record became one of the biggest sellers of 1968. Tiny had beaten Carson at his own game, and one would have expected ego-sensitive Carson to order that Tiny Tim never return. Carson proved to be the good sport he appears to be on television, and Tiny Tim came back to *Tonight* for a visit every two months or so.

Tiny Tim was making $50,000 a week, and the *Tonight Show* production staff knew they had hooked up with a sensation. The staffers also believed that Tiny Tim could serve as just the publicity gimmick they needed in the war against the myriad challengers that were barking up the *Tonight* tree. It was on the show that Tiny Tim announced his engagement to his girlfriend, Victoria Budinger, whom he referred to as "Miss Vicki."

Carson offered *The Tonight Show* to Tiny for his wedding. Although producer Rudy Tellez said that it was pre-arranged, Tiny Tim said he didn't know anything about the offer before Carson made the sudden invitation. "If someone came in beforehand, I don't remember," Tiny explained. "He said NBC would take care of all the bills and pay for Miss Vicki's wedding gown. That was the key phrase. The only thing he said was, 'I can't do it on Christmas because I'll be away.' We both agreed on the seventeenth of December."

Things were not happy with the couple, however. Tiny Tim did not believe Miss Vicki loved him, and he began to hear sleazy rumors about her. "If there was no Johnny Carson, there would have been no wedding," Tiny admitted years later. He would not have gone through with it, but he did not want to disappoint Carson or Vicki.

Evidently Budinger was none too thrilled to be married on *The Tonight Show*. "You better tell Mr. Carson you don't mean it, because I'm not going on television," she remembered saying.

The *Tonight Show* wedding went ahead, and the night of the wedding—December 17, 1969—became one of the most-watched late-night television events ever. Tickets for the studio audience that night had been a hot commodity. Carson's other guests, Florence Henderson and Phyllis Diller, had both dressed formally for the occasion, as had McMahon and Carson himself. Carson built up suspense for the wedding as long as possible by chatting with his other guests first. Finally, Carson announced, "And now here's the moment you've been waiting for."

The set had been decorated for three days for the auspicious event. The wedding was held in a mock-Eighteenth Century style. When the ceremony was complete, Carson gabbed with the newlyweds. Tiny thanked everyone for the free goods and services. He had been given many many gifts, but they were stolen. Tiny Tim never even received the videotape of the wedding he had been promised.

The marriage was the beginning of the end for Tiny Tim; America had had enough of the fad after the wedding. Tiny was booked a few more times on *The Tonight Show*, but it was over. His last real visit was in '71. He did return in '79, but that was charity. Vicki left him, and Tiny Tim was forced to play circus gigs.

Carson didn't even play highlights of the wedding in his annual anniversary gala show that year. "He wanted out," Tiny said. "He didn't want to be connected with the wedding." What had seemed a tasteful ratings event with a popular star soon looked like what it was, a cheap stunt cashing in on a fad.

The Tonight Show Goes West

After the Tiny Tim incident, the '70s had begun and the turbulent end of the '60s ushered in a new mindset with the new decade. The baby-boomers, who had been children when Carson began on *Tonight*, were adults now and watching him themselves. The Golden Age of television—the 1950s and early to mid 1960s—had passed. The show could've stagnated and died, but it changed with the times.

It was no longer live from a New York theater. The entertainment industry had almost altogether abandoned the Big Apple. Hollywood had become America's fantasyland, and the New York based *Tonight* was having trouble booking celebrity guests who had relocated to the West. *The Tonight Show* moved with them, and, at first, Carson wasn't pleased. Tellez remembered, "Johnny had said, 'I'm never leaving New York. I love it. I'll never move to California. Those people are weak. They have no books to read. It's awful.'" Carson was especially turned off on California because it was where he had first gone to earn stardom after he left Nebraska twenty years before. California had not embraced the young, struggling Johnny Carson; New York had, and Carson was set on the road to legend when he began hosting *Who Do You Trust?*.

The die was cast when Fred de Cordova replaced Tellez as executive producer. Tellez's contract wasn't renewed, and he left in '71. de Cordova was Mr. Hollywood. He had produced twenty films, his most well-known being *Bedtime for Bonzo* with Ronald Reagan. de Cordova had also served as the legendary Jack Ben-

ny's producer and director. de Cordova and his wife Janet were entrenched in the Hollywood social scene. As one journalist put it, "The de Cordovas attended A-list parties in Hollywood. Freddy and Janet had a reputation for knowing where to go, when to arrive, when to leave, skimming the top of the frivolities. The reputation was so well-established that it became the basis for an apocryphal story."

de Cordova was never one of the Golden Age visionaries, but one of the Los Angeles smooth-set professionals—all glitter, very little gold. Unlike previous *Tonight* producers, however, de Cordova wasn't building his career as he was building the show. He was already established, already sure of himself. Although he is exceedingly deferential to Johnny Carson's stardom in public, de Cordova would not be bullied by Carson. He quietly and competently went about managing the show, but with little of the innovation Rudy Tellez or Art Stark, had brought. Craig Tennis described de Cordova as "having a talent for charm which is almost staggering. He is also dictatorial, unpredictable, mercurial, and perhaps the most opportunistic human I have ever met."

de Cordova also became the longest running producer in *Tonight Show* history. He joined the crew in 1970, and remained for twenty-two years, until Carson himself stepped aside. Although Ed McMahon was Carson's sidekick in the viewing public's eyes, in reality it is obvious Fred de Cordova truly became Carson's right-hand man.

de Cordova wanted the show moved, so the show moved. Explaining the relocation, Carson said, "The main reason is the talent pool. There's not much television in New York anymore. When you do five shows every week for a year, it's a little sticky sometimes to find a large number of lively people in New York." When Carson said "lively people," he meant *famous* lively people, the kind provide the new smooth glitz of the show. No longer was it *The Tonight Show* most Americans grew up on, the smart glamour of the '50s and '60s, but a *Tonight Show* for the changing times.

The relocation began as a few temporary trips to the Coast, like those Larry King occasionally does for his CNN show, but the change-of-venue became permanent in 1972. The irony is that the man who orchestrated the change, Fred de Cordova, was a social friend of Carson and wife Joanne before joining *Tonight*, and that it was Joanne who suggested to her husband that he make de Cordova the new producer.

In the early '70s, however, the Carsons' marriage had fallen apart while they still lived in New York. Joanne had caught Johnny fooling around with a secretary; Carson, in turn, discovered Joanne's "love-nest" apartment in Manhattan. Carson wanted out, but was in despair over his second failure at marriage. He locked her out of their UN Plaza apartment. "He didn't want any part of Joanne anymore, yet he missed the companionship," said Trudy Moreault, a neighbor and mutual friend of the separated couple.

A divorce was decreed in '72, and Carson paid his second ex-wife several hundred thousand dollars in settlement and alimony. He was bitter, and began the ex-wife jokes in his monologue, only encouraging the tabloids' portrayal of Carson as a marital disaster.

Carson put the divorce behind him, moved West, and bought the Bel Air home he lives in today, the palatial estate previously owned by film magnate Mervyn LeRoy and his wife Kitty. He also met Joanna Holland, and soon rumors spread of another Carson marriage.

16

The Carson Decade

Since the beginning, every year Johnny Carson has celebrated his *Tonight* anniversary with a special program on October 1. For his sixth anniversary, in 1968, Carson pointedly ignored the Tiny Tim wedding which should have taken center stage with all the hype which had surrounded it.

October 1, 1972 served as the milestone for a decade of late-night Johnny Carson. NBC moved Carson to prime time for his tenth celebration. He had become a fixture in those ten years, and the industry knew it. President Richard Nixon sent his regards; Ronald Reagan, then California's governor, made an appearance by helicopter. Jack Benny, George Burns, and Jerry Lewis were guest luminaries, underlining the auspiciousness of the moment.

That Benny appeared was interesting. He was *the* classic comic of radio and early television, and as such, influenced Johnny Carson from the beginning, but eventually, Carson's stature began to eclipse Benny's. Carson recalled, "Many people say some of my mannerisms are like Jack's. Well, I think *all* comedians have 'ears'. They pick up, mimic, and eventually fall into certain patterns. I realize now that, in the early days of my career, I *was* too much like Jack. I tried to emulate him, which was wrong. But I *idolized* Jack. He had more influence on me than say, Bob Hope, who is a joke-teller, a one-liner.

"Most of all, from the standpoint of timing and structure," he continued, "Jack was a key influence on me. Basically, I, like

him, am a reaction comedian. I play off of the things that are happening around me. That is what works for me on *The Tonight Show*. When things happen around me, I can play off them by reaction, timing, pauses, and looks.

"When Jack had guest stars, he stood back, gave them the best material, and never was bothered when they got most of the laughs. He realized instinctively that it only strengthened him. But, in truth, there are very few comics who could have stood it. Most of them want and *need* all the funny lines for themselves.

"Most comedians are, by nature, very mercurial, especially in their anger, but not Jack. I never saw him display any temperament. He was the most disciplined performer I ever met. Overall, Jack seemed to be a very secure man.

"Performers like Jack, who sustain over the years, are the ones people identify with—as a person as well as an entertainer. I have seen a lot of clever performers come and go simply because the audience just didn't like them, didn't care about them. Jack's audiences always cared.

"Jack never acted like he had a superior quality. That's why everyone could identify with him. It may sound dull to keep praising him, to make him sound so saintlike. People always look for *something* in a life like Jack's. But, with Jack, what it comes down to is *the man was what he was*."

It's no surprise Carson revered Benny above all others. In some ways, Carson *was* Benny; in others, he *wanted to be* Benny, but couldn't. They shared sustainability, Carson never came across on *The Tonight Show* with a superior quality. His banter with guests was razor-sharp, but they generally began on a level playing field.

Carson might have praised Benny's security, his ability to give his guests the best lines, his even temper, but Carson could find none of these qualities within himself. Carson would give others some good opportunities, but when a guest began to get more popular than the host, Carson would shoot them down to keep the spotlight on himself. It's been a recurring problem over the years that if Carson noticed any of the other show regulars getting more attention than himself—most notably with McMahon—he would blast them later to keep them in their place. It illustrates a temper in Carson, but it's more. "'Don't ever put that shit on the show again,' he'll scream," said one *Tonight* staffer. "And then Carson will rant about how inept some of the other guests were."

One incident tells the Johnny Carson/Jack Benny story better than anything else. It was a conversation that night between Carson and Jack Benny, himself a legend. Journalist Laurence Leamer reported, "'Remember some time ago you were the toastmaster at a testimonial dinner for me?' Jack Benny asked as he sat on-stage at Johnny's primetime tenth-anniversary show. 'At this dinner I said that for many yea*I've* been Johnny Carson's idol.'

"'It's true,' Johnny said, looking at the aging comedian who was an authentic show-business legend.

"'And all of a sudden the whole thing switched,' Benny said, not a trace of humor in his voice. Benny stopped a moment, longer than any other comedian would have dared to pause. 'And you want to know something. It's not as much fun this way.'

"Johnny still idolized Benny, but *The Tonight Show* host himself was reaching semilegendary status." If he was "semilegendary" at his tenth, he would have made it all the way by his twentieth.

October 1 would become yet another anniversary for Carson. It had been the day he married Jody Wolcott in Nebraska in 1949, and at the tenth anniversary party after the *Tonight Show*, Carson revealed that he had married his third wife, Joanna, privately earlier that day. At that, an eleven-foot-tall wedding cake was wheeled out and the band struck up "Anniversary Waltz". Several of the celebrities present said kind words to Carson, and apparently, with real honesty, he responded, "I hope I never get too sophisticated and too involved to say I don't appreciate all this. I never thought I'd reach the point in my life when I would have this measure of success, and to have these people say all these things. It's really what it's all about and I thank you."

The Saturday Night Feud

NBC broadcast new *Tonight Show*s weeknights, Monday through Friday, at eleven thirty at night, Eastern time, whether Johnny Carson was on or not. He had negotiated a generous schedule; he would appear three nights a week, four during the ratings "sweeps" periods in the Fall and Spring, with several weeks vacation. The show filled in with celebrity guest hosts, and while the guests were never as popular as Carson himself, they usually fared reasonably well.

Saturday nights were the real problem for the network. They had been rerunning old *Tonight Show*s, but the response was abysmal. Fewer than half of NBC's affiliates picked up the weekend rebroadcasts, the ratings dropped through the floor. It was humiliating for one of the most successful programs in television history. Although Carson had long ago waged battle with NBC for compensation for *Tonight* reruns, he wanted the embarrassment off the air.

Dick Ebersol, NBC's young late-night programming executive, and producer Lorne Michaels, seemed to solve that problem with *Saturday Night Live*. *Saturday Night Live* would be a comedy-variety show broadcast live from New York on Saturday nights during the timeslot the disastrous *Tonight Show* reruns had occupied. In many ways, it was a renaissance of the concept Steve Allen had used for his original *Tonight!* series, with an emphasis on variety comedy skits and a stable of regulars, a format altogether abandoned when lone wolf Carson came aboard.

Carson had wanted a Saturday night replacement for the failed reruns, but he was still nervous. He called a meeting between himself and Ebersol and Michaels. He didn't want competition from his own network, and he didn't want *Saturday Night* to take off and decide to expand beyond Saturday night. Also Ebersol and Michaels were countercultural baby-boomers, and the new show was going to be decidedly hip. Carson was not a has-been, but he wasn't of this new generation coming into its own, either. Carson wanted to attract younger viewers, wanted to be hip, but guests such as Bob Hope and Debbie Reynolds were not of the rock'n'roll youth.

"So you guys are going to be on one night a week, huh?" Johnny said. "Well, guys, I've heard about your show, and it has similarities to mine."

"What we have here is a comedy-variety show as opposed to a comedy-talk show," Ebsersol explained.

"Well, we have variety here, too," Carson rebutted. He felt that his monologue, his Carnac and Aunt Blabby skits, and the visiting comics and singers qualified his show as primarily "variety," when in fact it was mostly known for Carson sitting behind a microphone talking to interesting people.

"You mean there's going to be no talk or interviews?" Johnny asked cautiously.

"None at all," was the reply.

When the new series debuted in 1975, it was a hit. It was daring, even a bit licentious, especially by Johnny Carson's standards. Having been raised and trained in the burlesque tradition, the risque was nothing new to Carson. In fact he had rankled his fair share of moralists in his day. Carson reveled in off-color, however he was suggestive, never blatant. *Saturday Night* was blatant, and heralded new, more open, standards of "decency" on television and in society.

George Carlin hosted the premiere. He said God was merely a "semisupreme being" because "everything He has ever made died." Chevy Chase did a sardonic newscast, saying of Gerald Ford: "If he's so dumb, how come he's president?"

On one show, Jane Curtain lampooned *The Tonight Show* itself, the sacred beacon of television entertainment. She was Chase's "co-anchor" in the "Weekend Update" mock newscast skit, and reported that *The Tonight Show* was returning to a live format, after "doing the show dead for fifteen years."

Johnny Carson was the King of Midnight, and the Not Ready for Prime Time Players on *Saturday Night Live* were in his late-night kingdom. The monarch was not amused. "I've seen some very clever things on the show and they have some very bright young people," Carson said. "But basically they do a lot of drug jokes, a lot of what I would consider sophomoric humor and a lot of stuff I find exceptionally cruel, under the guise of being hip . . . . One night the show ended a minute and a half early. There were eight people—eight people—standing there on-stage and not one of them could think of anything to say. They can't ad-lib a fart at a bean-eating contest."

The real star of *Saturday Night* was Chase; *New York* magazine called the young comedian the next Johnny Carson. The suggestion was that Chase replace Carson when the host retired. He responded, "I'd never be tied down for five years interviewing TV personalities."

Carson biographer Laurence Leamer put it this way, "Johnny was the establishment. The establishment always condemns the young for their bad taste and bad manners; what it fears is their youth, energy, and innovation. The young, for their part, imagine that they will never compromise, never settle into the routines of their elders."

Carson made a point of keeping *Saturday Night Live*'s regulars off his show. He would hype stars from competing networks night after night, but he wouldn't have on any of the stars from the new series which saved *The Tonight Show* from its Saturday night ignominy. Chase not only never succeeded Carson, he didn't appear as a guest until after he left *Saturday Night*. The late Gilda Radner didn't appear with Carson until 1983.

"It was trouble between me and Johnny," Chase later admitted. "It was not because we had any anger or rancor between us. Nobody ever came to me to talk about taking over *The Tonight Show*. It was just always in the press. At that time I didn't feel that hosting *The Tonight Show* was the direction I was going in, and I didn't voice it in a nice way. All I had to do was write Johnny a letter, apologizing for any remarks I may have made, and say, 'I think you're great,' and say, 'I want to be on the show.'"

By that time, all the young mavericks from *Saturday Night* had gotten older. Many had become movie stars. Chase was winning roles as older, establishment yuppies. He finally got his chance to sub for Carson in 1986, and what he had once dismissed, he realized first-hand was extremely difficult and required real talent. "It was very tough to be the guest host," Chase remembered. "I had just come out of a rehabilitation clinic, and I was a little nervous.

"The monologue was tough, because I had never done one in my life. I had put it together very fast. The most difficult were the interviews. Johnny has a philosophy about his guests. It's basically if you make your guests look good, you look good. I tell you, it's tough. He listens very carefully and he responds well, and he has obviously caught the heart of Middle America. It's tough."

Paul Corkery, another Carson biographer, says that now Carson and Chase play poker together. Corkery said, "Johnny really doesn't hold a grudge."

18

Maturing in the '70s

The late 1960s and early 1970s were kind of an "adolescence" for Johnny Carson's *Tonight Show*. It was learning and growing, but had its awkward moments as well; the Tiny Tim wedding perhaps the most glaring awkward moment. The move to California was growth.

Carson came into his own as an entertainer to reckon with when he successfully satirized the Watergate scandal. He had as much to do with Richard Nixon's downfall as did Woodward and Bernstein. "Mr. Carson alone presides over our consciousness," said *The New York Times* after the scandal was over. "When *he* began making Watergate jokes, we knew it was permissible to ridicule the President, that Mr. Nixon was done for....Johnny Carson is crystallized cynicism. Such, too, seems to be the mood of his constituency."

Carson's greatest talent is his ability to read an audience, to know what they will go for, what will get a laugh, what won't. "I think our studio audience is a good barometer of how the country is feeling," Carson explained. "Five hundred people can give you a pretty accurate indication; you can see right away what is fair game. When Agnew first got started, and nobody had heard of him, he was a great target for jokes. Then when he was in trouble, you could see that a lot of people were pretty hard hit by that in Middle America."

Johnny Carson celebrated his twelfth anniversary with *The Tonight Show* in '74; NBC placed a large ad in *The Los Angeles*

Times, applauding him "on the twelfth anniversary of the longest-running and most successful late-night entertainment series in the history of network television." Carson once again did his two-hour primetime anniversary special, with NBC president Bob Howard making an appearance.

The executive's flattery of Carson on the air did nothing to hinder his desire for a bigger salary when he negotiated his next contract in '76, a year before the previous agreement was to expire. Carson landed $3 million a year, thanks to Henry Bushkin, the Carson's divorce attorney of a few years prior; Bushkin had crafted the settlement with Joanne. The lawyer became a valued advisor and friend to Carson for several years; Carson began calling him "Bombastic Bushkin" on the show.

Perhaps the greatest mark of the importance of Johnny Carson and *The Tonight Show* was competitor ABC's invitation to host the Oscar Awards presentation in 1978. The job of Oscars host was usually reserved for movie stars, normally seen as a cut above television stars. For Carson, a television star, to host the movie people's sacred night, was monumental. For his part, he added a bit of irreverence to an otherwise stuffy occasion—"Two hours of sparkling entertainment, spread out over four hours," he called the show. The awards program ratings were higher in '78 than they had ever been, and Carson was asked back the next year.

Courtship by a rival network fueled the fire that culminated in the *Tonight Show* crisis which would end the decade. Carson had just negotiated a contract which gave him $3 million, fifteen weeks of vacation time, and a three-day work week except during sweeps periods in which he worked four days a week.

Before, it had been Carson who had been unhappy with a deal after it had been struck and wished to renegotiate. This time, he was quite satisfied with the arrangement, but the network had second thoughts. Ratings for *The Tonight Show* had begun to drop because of Carson's many absences, and NBC's total profit was down twenty percent, which had more to do with the their pathetic primetime line up of series such as *BJ and the Bear* and *Sheriff Lobo* than with *The Tonight Show*.

Fred Silverman, NBC president, went to Carson, the network's heavy hitter, as the solution to the whole problem. He told *Newsweek*, "It doesn't take a mastermind to figure out that when Carson is on the program does better than when he isn't on. He has a contract permitting him to make only three appearances each week, and that has only a couple more years to run. But I only hope there will come a moment in time when he will say to himself, 'I love *The Tonight Show*, and I'm going to do a little bit more.' He's a very competitive and professional guy. I don't think he must enjoy reading that the thing is slipping."

Silverman's patronizing attitude infuriated Carson and the host began to make NBC and Silverman jibes in his nightly monologue. Carson was also unhappy with Silverman's attempt to pressure him to book more guests from NBC's failing shows. Carson didn't want to use his talent and celebrity to float losers. Finally, he had enough of Fred Silverman and the network. He announced he would be quitting *The Tonight Show* on rival CBS' *Sixty Minutes* program. The NBC News people couldn't even find their own star for an interview. Carson said he was "emotionally and intellectually tired and wanted to pursue other interests including primetime variety shows, movies, and more personal appearances and concerts."

Caught flatfooted with egg on his face, Fred Silverman issued a public plea for Carson to remain on the show. Joanna Carson said, "Johnny was at a point. He wanted to do everything throughout his life. He was offered a lot of roles to star in movies. At that point, perhaps, he thought he needed a new challenge."

There was still ABC's card to be played. *People* magazine said, "It doesn't take Karnak the Magnificent to guess what might be in the envelope ABC proffered Carson: whatever he wants." ABC allegedly offered Carson the opportunity to make appearances on specials, and more importantly, become a full-time producer on his own.

Carson said he wanted to leave NBC within a few months, to quit the contract which obliged him to stay with *The Tonight Show* two more years. NBC said they expected Carson to honor his contract.

In the end, it wasn't the network who convinced Carson to stick with it. It wasn't his wife, and it wasn't even his old stage partner, Ed McMahon. The one force which kept a disgruntled Johnny Carson on the NBC gravytrain was the real power behind *The Tonight Show*, executive producer Freddie de Cordova.

19

de Cordova's Magic

When Carson returned to the show from vacation on May 1, 1979, he announced that he was remaining on *The Tonight Show*, but made it clear Silverman's bullying had nothing to do with his decision. Carson said the reversal was "definitely not due to any pressure from network execs. I feel I owe it to the show and to NBC."

"When Johnny decided to stay with NBC, it was the right decision because when you're 'king of the network,' you don't switch in midstream," Joanna Carson commented. "Johnny always made the right decision when it came to his career."

At a roast for Carson a few weeks later, Bob Hope quipped, "I can admire a man who can do what John has done to his network as many times, as many ways, and in as many positions. Next year he's got a sweeter deal: $43 million and he only has to show up once a week to pick up his messages."

Evidently, Freddie de Cordova and his wife Janet took the Carsons to dinner and impressed upon Carson that an antagonistic exit would not be the best move. For de Cordova to have talked Carson out of his most serious threat of retirement to date was a coup. It certainly proved de Cordova's clout, even at an advancing age. Carson himself sees and appreciates that power. "I didn't take on Freddie just to blow smoke," Carson said.

de Cordova managed *The Tonight Show* evenly and steadily, making sure everyone—stage hands, writers, and Carson alike—kept to the job at hand. "I'm chief traffic cop, talent scout,

number one fan and critic all rolled into one," de Cordova explained. A *People* reporter said of de Cordova: "If *The Tonight Show* is, as observers often suggest, a sort of living room on the air, there's no question that the living room isn't Johnny's alone."

Fred de Cordova was born in New York City, the son of a "shrewd, maybe a trifle shady" Portuguese businessman. His family was on a financial roller coaster, which de Cordova said "gave me a desire always to be on salary. The highs never made up for the lows."

He graduated from Northwestern University, attended Harvard Law School, but was sucked into the world of show business when John Shubert, a classmate related to the theatrical family, offered him a job as a stage manager. de Cordova tried his hand at acting, but "I decided I could do less damage behind the camera," he stated.

His social career has, over the years, become more well-known than his professional. He was a bachelor until the age of 53, and in his youth dated Joan Crawford, Ava Gardner, and Lana Turner. He married Janet shortly before joining *The Tonight Show*. de Cordova left movies, but remained friends with his *Bedtime for Bonzo* colleague, Ronald Reagan. The de Cordovas have been guests at the White House.

He moved to television, where he excelled. de Cordova was producer/director for *The Burns and Allen Show*, then for *The Jack Benny Show* for nine years. After retiring from *The Tonight Show*, it will still be for his proficient work on that show for which he will be best remembered. "I still get a high at the end of a great show," he said after fifteen years at the *Tonight* helm. After a show, de Cordova goes to Carson's dressing room for a drink and a postmortem.

Thanks to the efforts of de Cordova, the other staff, and Carson himself, his twentieth anniversary in '82 was yet another grand milestone. The audiences still lined up as early as seven in the morning to get their tickets, and across the nation, fifteen million viewers looked forward to the relief of Johnny Carson after the late news. Things weren't going as well for Johnny off the air.

20

Three Strikes

Johnny Carson's marriage to his third wife, Joanna, appeared to be the most stable and happiest of all, as if three was indeed Carson's lucky number. Carson infrequently mentioned his personal life on *The Tonight Show* in anything other than a humorous manner. He was too private and too much of a showman for that. Indeed, it was a tribute to his relationship with Joanna that he made one of his very few serious—and personal—statements on *The Tonight Show* on her behalf. His only other notable personal statement on the air came at the end of a program in the summer of 1991, when Carson said a few words about his son, Rick, who had died a short time earlier.

The tabloid *National Enquirer* put Carson on their cover in 1981 and printed an accompanying story alleging that his marriage had fallen apart. Carson was furious. He carried a copy of the newspaper on the show and said, "I hope you will indulge me in a few minutes of some personal comment. I have ambivalent feelings about what I'm going to say, and it has to do with *National Enquirer*. Somebody today handed me a copy of the *National Enquirer*.

"The reason I have ambivalent feelings about it is that I'm giving publicity to the publication of which I think stinks, number one. And the possibility I will give them more publicity and people will read the article whom otherwise might not have seen it.

"On the cover is my picture. Inside, the headline says 'Johnny Carson Marriage in Serious Trouble.' It says, 'close friends say he and wife Joanna are headed straight for divorce.'

Ed McMahon

"I have not seen this until this morning. Now, before I get into this or say anymore, I want to go on record right here in front of the American public because this is the only forum I have. They have this publication, I have this show.

"This is absolutely, completely, 100 percent falsehood. It's untrue for openers. I guess I should be used to this kind of stuff, being in the entertainment business as long as I have, but they also attacked my wife in this particular article.

"They said some very nasty things, attributed to her, again, close friends and pals. And when they attacked my wife, then I get a little bit angry . . . .

"Now, I could sue the *National Enquirer*. I'm not going to sue the *National Enquirer* because I don't want to go through the four or five years of litigation in which they call friends in and sources and put them through the mills. If you've ever been in deposition for this kind of thing, it's a very laborious task to go through.

"I'm not going to put my wife through it. My wife is a wonderful person. The comments they have made about her are completely untrue.

"The only reason I'm mentioning this, the people who want to believe it, fine. I don't care. But our friends, our relatives, our family, our children, our parents who read something like this . . . we've got calls already from all over the country, saying, 'I understand you're headed . . .' because they say you're going to get a divorce, and they go through a lot of other crap I'm not going to read to you.

"I'm going to call the *National Enquirer*, and the people who wrote this, liars. Now that's slander. They can sue me for slander. You know where I am, gentlemen.

"Please accept my invitation for calling you liars. I've done it publicly now in front of fifteen or twenty million people and I will be very happy to defend that charge against you."

With that, Carson finished. The studio audience applauded enthusiastically, and that was the end of that. The statement made headlines for days, but the *Enquirer* never did sue for slander. The episode was very much like what Jack Paar might have done on his own *Tonight Show*.

That the studio audience and public opinion in general came to Carson's side following this tirade says something about the power of his television program; it says something about the sense of intimacy created between Carson and the audience, a sense of intimacy that the *Enquirer* could never create between itself and its own audience. "He comes to [the audience] at the most vulnerable time of their lives—when it's dark, when it's late, when they could be lonely or ill," Joanna explained.

The on-air invective should also say something about Carson's relationship with that woman. Johnny and Joanna Carson were in love for so many years, and were married for ten years before the marriage finally did in reality fall apart. They seemed to be true partners. Carson talked very fondly of her everywhere, and for her part, Joanna wanted to share her life with Carson, her excitement.

For instance, Carson had never travelled much. Before Joanna, he had been abroad once perhaps. For all his fame and fortune, Carson was still a simple Nebraskan at heart. Joanna, on the other hand, had been a successful model and was more worldly. She demonstrated her love by sharing her enthusiasm for travel. "Our first trip to Europe was probably in 1974. We started to go to the south of France, and Johnny became very interested in tennis," Joanna Carson explained. "And we used to go to Wimbledon, in London, for the tennis matches every year, and then travel to the south of France before coming home.

"One year I promised him I was going to take him to Italy, and we went. It was in 1980 and we had a wonderful time. We flew to Rome and did all the things that people do in Rome for the first time—we saw the Vatican and went to the Borghese Gardens and ate pasta and drank wonderful wine and sat in the plazas. And then we drove from Rome to Ravello, and we stayed with Gore Vidal and Howard Austin in Ravello. Then we went to Capri on the hydrofoil—and that was something I always wanted to do with Johnny. It was a very special time for me because I never thought I'd get him there. And I remember that we got off the hydrofoil and looked at the funicular railway that goes up the side of the mountain, and he couldn't believe what was going on and I said to him, 'I got you here, and I'm so happy.'"

Back at home, however, problems between the two began. Joanna originally had not wanted to move from New York to California with the show because she thought it would be too "tacky." Once she was there, however, she settled right in, almost too well for Carson. She soon assimilated into the Beverly Hills social set. "Johnny had to push and shove to get her to come to California in 1972," said one Carson friend. "Joanna insisted she wouldn't like it, but she took to the life very well."

One prominent Beverly Hills resident said of Joanna, "An awful lot of people could be very jealous of Joanna—she's beautiful, brilliant, and is very loyal. She's also very organized and is a fantastic businesswoman."

It was those business instincts that got Joanna Carson involved in managing charity organizations. She became president of SHARE: Share Happily and Reap Endlessly—one of the largest, which assists retarded children. Another unnamed associate remarked, "Joanna is Sicilian, a bundle of emotion. She can be very sweet or very rough. She was always determined to be somebody. In SHARE it was the same thing. She was determined to become president of SHARE, and she did. She's very domineering, even a little cynical . . . ."

Much of Joanna's work involved social galas and glitzy entertaining. She roped Johnny Carson in from the first, and had her famous husband emcee a SHARE banquet. At the party, he quipped, "I was invited here in the same manner that Agnew was invited to return the money."

It was obvious Carson wanted to have nothing to do with the jet-set social scene. He was private, quiet. After all, he exhausted all of his sociability at work on *The Tonight Show*. Why did he need to worry about Beverly Hills parties with a few social-climbing guests, when he had a national party with millions.

"I remember an episode a few years ago that illustrates Joanna's domineering streak," recalled another unnamed friend. "It was at a SHARE party. Johnny was to be the master of ceremonies, and Governor Jerry Brown was outside the building and was delayed coming in. Joanna made Johnny stand there on-stage for twenty minutes, with really nothing to do, until Brown made his entrance. He could have sat down. But Joanna wouldn't let him. She wanted him standing for the governor. He looked glum. She just held on to him, and made him stand there, until Brown came in. He looked foolish. But it was the sort of thing she'd do. She's tough and liked wielding power."

"The problem with Joanna is that she loved parties and Johnny hated them," another Carson companion said, putting the whole thing best. "Johnny isn't reclusive, he's just a bit of a loner. He loves astronomy and has a couple of telescopes in his living room. He also has a complete Nautilus gym and works out every day. He loves to read. He's a big reader. And he loves going to art shows. But most of all he loves *The Tonight Show*. Being out every night [at Joanna's functions] took away from the energy."

"Oh it sure was a good marriage for the most part," Joanna later said. But she went on to add, "Around 1980, I began to see things in our marriage that I didn't understand. Changes in Johnny that I didn't understand."

Despite rumors and the *Enquirer* blow-up, the Carsons attempted to work out their problems. "Johnny would discuss the issues," Joanna remembered. "We just couldn't resolve them. I used to say to him, 'If you would devote as much time to our relationship, our marriage, to your family, as you devote to that show, you couldn't help but have a 'hit' on your hands."

While Joanna Carson was very involved in outside social functions, she was also deeply focused on family, hers and Carson's. When Carson's parents were alive in the '80s and moved from Nebraska to retirement in Scottsdale, Arizona, it was Joanna who decorated her parents-in-law's home, partially from the furnishings from her own Fifth Avenue apartment.

She even got a surprising "thank you" call from Carson's first wife, Jody, the mother of his three sons. "I remember particularly Jody called me one evening, out of a clear blue sky, and she thanked me! She kept me on the phone a long time, thanking me. I said, 'Jody, for what? Why are you thanking me?'

"She said, 'I'm thanking you because you're giving my boys back to me.' I thought that was a very interesting remark, because I always told the boys they had to be concerned about their mother, they must be concerned with their mother, what she was doing and so forth.

"I think [they did] not see her often as [they] should have, but then this strong, principled person was saying to them, 'You must care for your mother . . . you must call her on the holidays—it's Mother's Day . . . .'"

That kind of family feeling made Carson the traditional Nebraskan happy. "It was a very good marriage for most of the time," Joanna said later. "He used to talk about it on the show all the time—'This was it.' But we just couldn't resolve the problems that arose. I think we tried for a year and a half, and ultimately I didn't want to lose respect and wake up in the morning and not like me, because I like me a lot . . . . I think somewhere along the way, you try so hard, you try to resolve things when . . . I just kind of lost respect for him."

When Carson's previous marriage, to Joanne Copeland, perished, it was Carson who ordered Joanne away and locked her out. With strong-willed Joanna, it was the other way around. She recalled, "So I made the decision that this marriage was not going anywhere, was not continuing in the manner it should, especially with all the time put into it! So I asked Johnny to leave the house, to go to our beach house and stay there.

"I think there was a certain shock, a certain anger—it hurts the male ego—and that's when the stories started that the whole thing was about money. That's when the press started perceiving me as greedy, as going after the pockets of the man that I loved. That was outrageous. Money was never even a subject that came up in our marriage. It hurt me badly; money had nothing to do with the end of our marriage."

Money might not have been an issue during the union, but it certainly became one during the separation and divorce. Joanna worked with her lawyer to craft a deal with Carson. To begin with, they drew up a budget of her Beverly Hills lifestyle during her marriage to Carson, which came to $220,000. This was not supposed to be a proposal, just a figure to work from. The media took this sizable amount and had a field day. "All of a sudden these stories started to appear, and everyone starts asking me what about this $220,000 maintenance fee or whatever you want to call it. This was outrageous. Apparently, they took this number, and the press took this number, and that's what I'm asking for, when in fact it wasn't what I was asking for."

The third former Mrs. Carson saw it as a calculated move by Carson's lawyer and close friend at the time, Henry Bushkin, to disparage her to swing a favorable divorce for Carson. "There was a campaign, a deliberate campaign—not so much on Johnny's part—to have Johnny be the hero and have me be the gal who done him wrong. Deliberate, no question about it," she said.

"I can only say I do know what I asked Johnny for in the presence of his lawyers and mine. They called him on the phone and told him the amount which I thought was a feasible amount to cover myself while we were going through these divorce proceedings.

"But he did not feel—and I never could figure out whether Johnny or Bushkin made the decision—it was right. They offered me $15,000 [a month]—take it or leave it. That's when I told the lawyers to go to court."

It was at this point when the ex-wives became an integral part of the Carson *Tonight Show* persona. *Tonight* viewers were bombarded daily with news of the divorce, and Carson didn't miss using juicy current events in his monologue, even if he was the subject. One night Carson said, "An old lady stopped me on the street on my way to the show.

"She says, 'Johnny, I want a divorce from you.' And I say, 'But we're not even married.' She says, 'Yeah, but I want to skip right to the goodies.'"

Another night, Johnny joked, "I went to see my butcher the other day, Murray Giblets. I said, 'How do I pick a good turkey?' And he says, 'You ought to know. You're a three-time loser.'"

It was all classic Carson, laughing at his own problems. It was the showman thing to do, and it brought him that much closer to the audience. People felt they were really getting to know Carson through his nightly conversations concerning his woes. Other comedians, friends of Carson, picked up on the jocularity and also began poking fun. "Johnny's greatest joy is finding new and talented young people and introducing them to fame and fortune. Unfortunately, most of them are his ex-wives," quipped Bob Newhart.

Joanna, however, felt that America was getting a rather one-sided impression of her marriage and her husband and stopped watching the show. She recalled, "It was very difficult for me to have a husband, and I think for the children to have a father, whom everybody emulated and loved and related to, and then when you saw the reverse side, you just wanted to say, 'Why? Why is that which everybody in the nation loves and gets, not there for me?'

"I was the one who was supposed to be the yelling, screaming Italian who would lose her temper, and the bottom line is that it was the reverse. Sometimes I was scared. I told him I was scared because sometimes when he drank, he was a totally different personality. There were times I was scared. And he does have a temper, flies off the handle. He has a very difficult time saying he's sorry.

"He wasn't like that from the beginning. Or at least it was something I didn't see. I would say that in late 1980 I started to see a definite change . . . . Something that I didn't understand." Whether that "something" was simply his growing displeasure with the social scene Joanna was forcing him into, or something entirely different, is unclear.

The judge presiding over the Carson divorce awarded Joanna $40,000 temporary support until a permanent deal was arranged. The $220,000-a-month figure still nagged at America. It translated to $2.6 million a year. Ellen Goodman, the syndicated columnist, provided a more sympathetic view. "The request for $2.6 million," Goodman said, "surely makes Joanna Carson a candidate for the hit parade of top ten spenders. But . . . someone should present the other side . . . . If the Carsons were still married, we would regard her as no more than the overindulged wife of an overindulged performer . . . . Is it more outrageous for Joanna to be awarded $220,000 a month . . . than for Johnny to be paid $1.5 million a month by NBC?"

Still, $220,000 wasn't even the true request. "I asked the judge for what was fair and not a penny more," Joanna defended. "I felt just terrible at the way I was portrayed."

When the final divorce came in August, 1985, she didn't get $2.6 million, but she got a lot more than the $15,000 a month Carson's people offered. She got the Bel Air LeRoy home, three cars, a healthy chunk of stock in Carson's corporation, as well as artwork and more than $2 million in cash spread over five years.

Carson was free of the binds of Beverly Hills socializing. De Cordova said, "Johnny doesn't need to go to other cocktail parties. *The Tonight Show* is his cocktail party. That's where he sparkles." Yet Carson was still unhappy at the marriage's end. At his last meeting with Joanna, when the paperwork was finalized, Carson told his new ex-wife, "What I'll miss most is not being able to talk to you."

Carson's Last Decade

The contract Johnny Carson settled with NBC in the late '70s giving him a three-day work week had been meant to allow him to spend more time with Joanna. Without Joanna, Carson gave himself more fully to his true mistress, *The Tonight Show*. He signed a deal to stay on into the 1980s, and agreed to a four-day work week. He also had the show cut from ninety down to sixty minutes a night.

The Tonight Show during the '80s wasn't changing with the times. The decade came in on disco and went out with rap and heavy metal, starting with John Travolta and ending with Mel Gibson. Many Carson guests were washed up has-beens that younger viewers barely recognized. *The Tonight Show*'s has had a difficult time catching up, with executive producer Fred de Cordova usually seen as the major culprit. "He only books people who will receive the approval of his 70-year-old friends in Beverly Hills," complained one former *Tonight Show* staff member.

de Cordova counters, saying he believes the audience likes proven stars, not "hot shots with one hit." That may be true, but when dutifully respectful and deferential pop singer Madonna was booked on the show, it was Carson that basked in reflected glory.

An Eddie Murphy *Tonight Show* appearance makes the point the best. Murphy was of the *Saturday Night Live* ilk that Carson had dismissed a decade earlier as "sophomoric" and "cruel." By the late '80s, however, he had become one of Hollywood's biggest stars with megahits such as the *Beverly Hills Cop* movies and his *Raw* concert film. Murphy appeared on the show in '87 to promote the second *Cop* film, and brought along his friend Chris Jackson. Jackson was a young aspiring comedian himself, and did a Prince impression that Murphy called "the funniest thing I've ever seen."

Murphy walked on to the set to thunderous applause. Then it began. Carson asked nice, safe, pleasant questions, questions the young, black street comedian had no interest in answering. Carson biographer Laurence Leamer recalled the incident: "'What were you doing ten years ago?' Johnny asked.

"'Stealin' somebody's bike.'

"'Do you remember?' Johnny asked, as if he hadn't heard right.

"'Yeah, I'm twenty-six and we'd go and steal bikes,' Murphy said. Then he looked out into the audience. 'Remember and they caught us and . . . .' Murphy was talking to his friends as if Carson was an unwanted observer. 'Not Woody. Whose mother came . . . .'

"'Did you bring a *gang* with you here tonight?' Johnny asked.

"'I brought my *friends.*'

"'Are you pretty much of a loner?'

"'I'm not a loner at all. I'm telling you, we walked in the place today and you should have saw the people in the back saying, 'Who are all these Negroes coming in?'

"The audience exploded in laughter.

"'What's interesting is that it was Floyd, the shoeshine man, who said that,' Johnny said, referring to one of the few blacks at NBC.

"Murphy laughed as if amused at something besides Johnny's joke. After the showing of a clip of *Beverly Hills Cop II*, the comedian's stint with Johnny was about up. Johnny asked a few last questions about Murphy's sudden wealth.

"'You know what I'm saying,' Johnny said. 'You walk down the street and you see something in the store window and you say, 'Man, look at that.'

"'I do that sometimes.'

"'Now what catches your eye?' Johnny asked, leaning toward Murphy, who earned millions a picture. 'A watch? A coat?'

"Murphy was convulsing in laughter. 'What do you like? What catches your eye?' he said mimicking Johnny. 'Look at that shiny ring. Hey, Amos, get a load a that coat. That's a mighty big watch there.'

"'Hey, where's Chris Jackson at?' Murphy asked. 'Do you know a guy called Chris Jackson?'

"'Do I know who?' Johnny asked, momentarily bewildered. He had almost lost control of this interview, and now this.

"'Where's he at?'

"'Chris Jackson?' Johnny asked, looking around for help.

"'This guy does an imitation of Prince that is the funniest,' Murphy said as a tall, husky black man walked on-stage.

"'Is this Chris Jackson?' Johnny asked, as if it might be Lech Walesa or a member of the Vienna Boy's Choir.

"'Come here, Chris,' Murphy said.

"'Come here. I don't . . . I don't know,' Johnny stuttered. 'How're you doing?'

"'Everybody, Chris Jackson,' Murphy said, introducing his friend.

"Jackson got down on his knees. 'You don't have to be beautiful,' Chris sang. It was not exactly a world-class Prince imitation, but Murphy doubled up in laughter. Johnny laughed so hard, but abruptly ended the segment when Jackson finished and walked off-stage.

"Afterward, Jackson hid in the men's room, afraid that he was going to be thrown out. A band member happened upon the young comedian there. 'You were great,' he said. 'I've never seen that before.' Jackson decided it was okay to come out."

Indeed, the band member was right. It was a rare occurrence, but it would grow more and more common, if not always so brazen. Johnny Carson was struggling to be hip, but becoming a complete parody of himself. Murphy played it for all it was worth. It was not often the king lost control of his court. Carson was establishment, and those of Carson's generation were respectful of the establishment. Murphy and those like him were anti-establishment, interested in making their own rules. Those new rules were getting big laughs, perhaps bigger than Carson's, and the king was made out to be the court fool.

Showman or Businessman?

Carson decided to stay with *The Tonight Show* past the '80-'81 season when a series of business dealings soured. He had run the company behind *The Tonight Show* for years. By the 1980s, Carson expanded his corporate holdings with the help of his friend and lawyer, Henry Bushkin.

Carson and Bushkin were close for years—it was said that the attorney had a phone in his office for Carson's calls only. Bushkin represented Carson's interests fiercely, not just as a client, but as a valued friend. Bushkin not only protected his friend in personal matters such as his last two divorces, but in his finances.

The attempted construction of a "Carson corporate empire" began simply enough when Bushkin was approached by Gordon Baskin, a prominent California businessman. KCOP-TV, an independent television station in Orange County, was up for sale. What better investment for a television star than a television station?

"I was invited to Carson's home," Baskin said. "I described the situation. Carson would at times be flippant, but he seemed incisive in his comments. We had found a station and a price. We had a verbal commitment from one of the biggest banks."

KCOP slipped away, but Baskin came back with KVVU-TV in Las Vegas. KVVU was another independent up for sale, this time for $5.5 million. According to the agreement, Carson would receive 90% of equity, Bushkin's law firm getting five percent, and Baskin getting the last five. Bushkin wanted to add minority partners for the tax breaks they would bring, so the deal was reconstructed and two Asian-American businessmen and a Mexican-American businessman were added.

Baskin smelled a rat from the beginning. "Never was I alone with Johnny Carson," Baskin revealed. "Henry wouldn't even go to the bathroom when I was there."

Baskin returned a year after the television deal was complete. He interested Bushkin and Carson in buying the Garden State Bank in Hawaiian Gardens in Los Angeles. This bank wasn't a pillar of the fiscal community. It had one branch far from Bel Air or Beverly Hills in one of the less affluent sections of the city. The bank only had about $11 million in assets, small for any bank. As if a sign from providence, however, the bank was located on Carson Boulevard.

The new partnership included Bushkin, Carson, Baskin, and a lawyer named Arnold Kopelson. It was the Carson connection that made the deal work. "The man was on TV every night," Kopelson observed. "We felt he would be a natural draw for the institution."

They secured a loan to purchase the bank, and immediately changed the name to the Commercial Bank of California because, as Carson quipped, the name Garden State "sounded like it was in New Jersey."

One journalist put it this way: "Los Angeles had 'in' automobiles, 'in' neighborhoods, 'in' restaurants, 'in' personal trainers, 'in' dog beauticians. Why not an 'in' bank for the big *machers* in the television and film industry? Even the less affluent mortals from Anaheim to Yuba City would be able to rub dollars with Johnny."

Carson was all spiffed up at the party celebrating the opening of the bank's new corporate headquarters on Sunset Boulevard in West Hollywood. Over 1,000 people flocked to Johnny Carson's bank opening. Carson even got his own desk and nameplate that read "John W. Carson." "I'm really enjoying this new adjunct to [show] business," he announced, "although I don't think I'll cause David Rockefeller to lose any sleep."

"Johnny did the bank to be one of the guys," said Fred Kayne, Carson's stock broker. "Other people were forming banks, and it was started with the best intentions."

Day to day operation of a bank was quite different from hosting a television program, and the new bank soon ran into problems. The bank loaned out 80% of its deposits in three months, but the deposits were in unstable certificates of deposit. There were millions in unsecured loans.

Gordon Baskin sent certified letters to all the bank board members, alerting them to his concern. "I just learned . . . that a new unsecured loan was made to the Bushkin, Kopelson firm in the amount of $160,000 at a favorable interest rate," wrote Baskin. "This is one of the largest loans in our portfolio. I am worried that it may represent an improper transaction under the sections of the Financial Code which forbid banks to make loans to directors, officers, or entities controlled by them." Baskin, a former bank official, advised that these improper loans be paid off.

Carson had gone to the initial board meetings and tried to follow the proceedings, but felt out of place, whispering to others to bring up what he believed important.

Baskin didn't feel he was listened to and resigned. He wanted to sell his shares in the investment corporation, but Bushkin pressured him to wait until the major holding, the Nevada television station, was sold. KVVU was bought for $5.5 million, and Gordon Baskin figured it had to be worth about $25 million when he wanted out. Carson's accounting firm, however, put the station on the auction block for a mere $2.9 million. Baskin felt he was being cut out and refused to sell his stocks in the station. The other partners, including Johnny Carson, filed suit and Baskin countersued.

In late 1984, Carson Broadcasting sold KVVU for $27.5 million, even higher than Baskin's estimate. This netted the other partners $8.66 a share, but the suit against Baskin went on. "The whole business really hurt," said Baskin later, looking back. "It took much out of my life. When you take on Johnny Carson, the most powerful person in this town, who would want to deal with you? It changed my life professionally and socially. Those were some years, just making a living."

For what it was worth, Gordon Baskin won his countersuit and received $2 million. Henry Bushkin and the other partners tried an unsuccessful appeal. Carson, all the while, was playing up his entree into the world of finance, calling Bushkin "Bombastic Bushkin" on *The Tonight Show* and joking that Bushkin was trying to get him to invest in such get-rich-quick-schemes as "Ronald Reagan Memory Schools."

It was no laughing matter when Carson's bank was connected to organized crime. The Commercial Bank made one of its first loans to a Jack Catain, Jr. Catain was president of Rusco Industries, and, as one former Treasury agent said, "As far as organized crime in Los Angeles, Catain was as big as they come. He was laundering money, passing cashier's checks in the Cayman Islands, extortions, all kinds of operations."

Rusco had been under investigations for organized crime for years. When they tried to buy a racetrack in Detroit, the *Free Press* found connections between the track and the mob. Catain responded with "I don't know and I couldn't care less."

Catain was referred to the Commercial Bank by Henry Bushkin. The Commercial Bank went so far as to throw a party in Catain's honor to show their appreciation for his business. Catain didn't invite Johnny Carson to the party, but instead, Ed McMahon.

Even while their investments stood on shaky ground, Bushkin and Carson made another purchase, another television station; this time KNAT in Albuquerque, New Mexico in 1982. The investors were not just bankers and brokers. The investment team for KNAT included a Hollywood roster. Carson took 41%; the playwright Neil Simon took 26%; 10% went to the singer Paul Anka (whose *Tonight Show* theme has been his own thirty year investment); Joan Rivers took four percent; and an up-and-coming comedian named David Letterman took five. In three years, they all lost $6 or $7 million and the station closed down before it was sold in 1985.

In what would have been a comedy-of-errors had it not been so expensive, Carson and Bushkin's second get-rich-but-lose-your-shirt-in-the-end plot was real estate development in Houston, Texas. Bushkin put together Carson, Neil Simon, and Simon's wife at the time, actress Marsha Mason, and several lawyers to invest in land for a luxury hotel. Carson travelled to the Lone Star State to put his showman's touch on the project, but as a reporter pointed out, "But before an acre could be sold, the Houston boom busted, and another luxury hotel was about as needed as a dry well."

Simon and Mason sued Henry Bushkin's firm, charging he had failed "to adequately investigate the transactions, to adequately document the transaction, to adequately explain . . . the risks . . . and to adequately advise . . . of their interest in the transactions or of the conflicts of interest created thereby." The complaint was dropped when Bushkin compensated the couple for their losses, leaving the remaining partners, including Carson, a bigger loss.

Carson and Bushkin's biggest folly was the attempted purchase of the Aladdin casino in Las Vegas. It seemed like a bright idea that Carson, a Vegas veteran entertainer, have his own casino, but Carson would be connected to organized crime in this venture, as well. The Aladdin had allegedly been run by mob families in Detroit and St. Louis. Carson's own opener when he did shows there, the singer Phyllis McGuire, was going with Mafia boss Sam Giancana.

The Nevada Gaming Commission would be very choosy who it let buy a lucrative casino. Bushkin hooked Carson up with

Edward Nigro, an experienced casino manager. They offered a down payment of $20 million. The Kinney corporation was ahead of the Carson team, however, in the Aladdin bidding. Bushkin arranged a merger of the Kinney offer with Carson's. The idea of a Johnny Carson's Aladdin seemed in the bag.

Kinney withdrew, possibly for lack of funds, possibly to avoid the embarrassment of a turn-down by the Gaming Commission. The owners of the Aladdin were desperate to sell, and Carson and Bushkin made another, slightly lower, offer. An obstacle developed in the form of Vegas singer Wayne Newton. "I think he tried to pull a cutesy publicity stunt," Carson said.

Carson had made fun of Newton for years on *The Tonight Show,* and Newton took it personally. One night in '73 Newton was watching Carson and Carson joked, "I saw Wayne Newton and Liberace together in a pink bathtub. What do you think that meant?"

The next afternoon, Newton stormed into Carson's office. "I remember what I told him almost verbatim," Newton recalled. "I said, 'I am here because I'm going through a personal dilemma in my life. I want to know what child of yours I've killed. I want to know what food of yours I've taken out of your mouth. I want to know what I've done that's so devastating to you that you persist in telling fag jokes about me.'

"Carson's face went white. He said, 'Well, Wayne, I don't write these things.' I told him I'd feel better if he did, and he asked me why. I said, 'Because at least it would mean that you're not the puppet I think you are, and that you aren't just reading some malicious lines written by some writer who crawled out from under a rock. I'm telling you right now: it better f—-in' stop, or I'll knock you on your ass.

"He said, 'I promise you nothing was ever intended in a malicious way. I've always been a big fan.' And then he went through all this bullshit about how much he likes me. He just kept talking, and it was obviously a nervous apology—but he never again told Wayne Newton jokes."

The Carson negotiations fell through. "Mr. Bushkin reneged on his letter of intent," said David Huwitz, attorney for the sellers of Aladdin. Newton quickly drew up his own letter of intent and his manager hooked him up with experienced, and allegedly shady, casino management people. Singer Lola Falana, whose career was jump-started by *The Tonight Show,* was on the Newton team. She later said, "I never quite understood what happened. All I know is that my friendship with Johnny was over."

At the same time, the NBC News investigative team of Brian Ross and Ira Silverman began to examine Wayne Newton's ties to organized crime. They directly linked Newton to Guido Penosi, who was involved with the Gambino crime family, but the story was full of rumor and "unnamed sources."

Newton saw the report. "I couldn't believe that something like that could be on television," he said. "It was just that everything I had worked for in my entire life, the reputation I had built, never having taken a cent from anybody, never having hurt anybody, to the best of my knowledge, never, that these people could portray such a vicious lie. And I switched to see if it was on one of the other networks, and it wasn't then and it never had been, just on NBC."

Naturally, Newton believed Carson had put his network up to it. Within a day, he backed down on that claim. "If I accused him, I'd be as wrong as NBC was last night," he said. He believed Bushkin was behind it, though. Newton sued NBC and won $19.3 million in damages against the network and their two reporters. NBC appealed and the decision was cut to $6 million, but Newton felt vindicated, although he didn't mention anything about Johnny Carson.

Most of Carson's business ventures ended when he broke his professional and personal relationship with Henry Bushkin. Carson wanted to sell off his assets. Bushkin advised against it, but Carson was adamant. Bushkin began to sell, but at exorbitant prices. He asked $70 million for Carson Productions, which was ridiculous. A number of people called the lawyer incompetent after the series of business debacles he had dragged Carson through. *The Wall Street Journal* called the Carson/Bushkin break "one of the more unpleasant Hollywood splits since Lewis left Martin."

These business disasters prompted Carson to stay with *The Tonight Show*. He needed to make up for the losses he took under Bushkin's advice. More than that, his pride brought him back to the show. He had failed as a husband three times, and failed as a businessman with Bushkin, but he felt loved and in control in entertainment.

The Heir Apparent

Not all of Carson's business ventures crashed in burning flames. When Carson reduced *The Tonight Show* to an hour, something was needed to fill the lost time. NBC originally approached Steve Allen, the original "King of Midnight," to host a show following Carson's. Allen was reluctant, but Silverman, who was NBC president at the time, jumped at it. "Carson and Allen, back to back. I love the idea!" he said.

Carson, however, was "apathetic" in Silverman's words. Allen wouldn't be following Carson. Instead of a veteran, it was to be a newcomer. That newcomer was David Letterman. Letterman was a stand-up comic who had made a mark as a regular guest, and then as a guest host when Carson was away.

For the first few years, *Late Night With David Letterman* was compared with *America 2Night*, a parody of a talk show broadcast in the late '70s. Letterman insisted that while his show was different, it wasn't parody. "It was never our intention to satirize or parody a talk show. It's just that we have an hour of TV to do each night, and it's got to be a talk show, so what can we can do within that would make us laugh? It's just silly, goofy, additional behavior," he recalled.

In the eight years before *Late Night With David Letterman* debuted in '82, Tom Snyder's show had been coming on after *The Tonight Show* to only moderate success. *Late Night*, however, took off like a rocket. It was very different from *The Tonight Show*; it was irreverent, hip, a bit off-color. That Carson sup-

ported this effort when he had panned the same hip comedy in *Saturday Night* is surprising. Perhaps he began to see a need to appeal to the young.

At Letterman's *Late Night* debut, *Time* magazine described Carson's heir apparent as "tall, slim, and laid-back—indeed, almost supine, like a Perry Como on mescaline." Feminist Gloria Steinem, one of Letterman's early guests, called the comedian's style "found humor." Where Carson was simple and straightforward, Letterman was off-beat, surreal, sometimes bizarre. "I just want to make the show as playful as possible," he said, as if it were his manifesto.

The new show gained popularity quickly, with executives and viewers alike. It wasn't long until Tom Snyder became just another late night pretender. "*Late Night* is equalling Tom Snyder's ratings," Brandon Tartikoff, then NBC's programming chief said within a few weeks of the debut. "It's more popular with 18 to 24 year olds. We're very pleased with it."

"I wouldn't say we're king of the mountain," Letterman said humbly after celebrating more than seven years on the air. "And I'm not sure we were ever avant-garde. I think it's true in the early days we felt like we had to establish ourselves as being different, so maybe it was easier for us to do odd things and take more chances. I think the grind of doing a show every night makes you more inclined to say, 'Well, we did that before, we can do it again.' A certain inertia takes over. But what I think has come over the years is a more consistent spirit. We have more confidence now in what we do."

Letterman's basic attitude toward entertainment isn't built on shock value, but neither is it within an establishment. "I like having a camera in different locations and being able to talk with people there. And I always love it when the 'civilians' are able to do something that gets a huge laugh. I like it sometimes when things just don't work, and you're overwhelmed with this hopeless, giddy attitude."

Although David Letterman doesn't follow the establishment, he respects it and realizes that it is what got him into the business and on NBC. He revealed, "I've always been a big fan of Jack Paar's. I had met him, and he had invited me into his home a couple of times. I had always found him to be really interesting and still very energetic and dynamic, and I had wanted to get him on the show. But the response was that he had been advised by friends not to go on our show because we would make fun of him. I was saddened by that."

Letterman has had to deal with a perception that he's mean or difficult, that he prefers to belittle his guests. "I suppose I'm all of those things," he revealed, "but we never invite somebody on to demonstrate condescension—or condensation. If somebody comes on and is a bonehead and is loafing through an interview, I resent that, and maybe I will then go after them. But if you come on and are polite and well groomed and behave yourself, then've got nothing to worry about.

"I'm stunned at the number of people in show business who come on and don't seem to get that what we want from them is a performance, you know, tell us three stories about your life. Anybody who has been on this planet twenty years and doesn't have three stories, well they should re-examine what they're doing.

"It used to trouble me that people thought our sole purpose for being in business is to make fun of people. Unfortunately, there is no joke that does not make fun of somebody. I try to make it, as often as not, me or the show or somebody in our little group. So if we do say something that looks like we're making fun of somebody else, it's in the spirit of everything. But some people don't buy that. I know that some people can't stand me, and it troubles me because I think we're just trying to do the funniest show we know how."

He's a Paar fan, but it's from Carson he takes his cues. As a boy, Letterman began watching Carson after school on *Who Do You Trust?* He said, "First of all, personally, if it had not had not been for *The Tonight Show* and Johnny Carson, I wouldn't have a car—probably wouldn't have shoes. But the real reason I look up to the guy is the longer I do this, the more respect I have for him. Show me somebody else in the history of television who has not only survived but also dominated for a quarter of a century. I think if you don't have respect for that, there's something wrong with you.

"And he still makes me laugh. In fact, I don't even watch *The Tonight Show* because how good he is makes me nervous and insecure. I look at that show, and I say to myself, 'Yeah, see, you're no Johnny Carson.'"

When Letterman was tapped for the post-*Tonight* spot, his endeavor was supervised by Carson, under the auspices of Carson Productions. Naturally, two shows shown on the same network in tandem are coordinated so that a guest won't appear on both in close proximity. Carson has served as Letterman's patron.

Letterman admitted, however, that it was hard leaving the *Tonight Show* nest for his own haunts as a duke of late-night. "I didn't think I'd have a problem with interviews because I had hosted *The Tonight Show*," he admitted, "and there, if you just sit and follow the notes that the staff has prepared for you, you can do a pretty good interview.

"But for some reason, on this show I had a lot of trouble. I think I just was frightened that suddenly I had to perform as the host of my own show. I was intimidated by guests. So it took a while to overcome that. I remember at one point having a major shift of attitude. After two or three years, it didn't seem that we could do anything to improve the ratings. I can remember just feeling this frustration and despair and exhaustion, and it was kind of like—screw it. At that point I was able to relax more."

The atmosphere of *Tonight* and *Late Night* are similar; the desk, the chairs, all of those standards are there. He even has a sidekick. Unlike *Tonight* where the sidekick and bandleader are separate, *Late Night* rolls them together into Paul Shaffer. Letterman says Shaffer seems much more integral to the success of his show than McMahon is to Carson. "I have a great deal of respect for Paul," said Letterman, "and if he decided to quit the show, I don't know that I would continue without him. We're close; we chat every day before the show and after the show. I like him, and I think he's the best at what he does. But we're not best friends. I think it would be odd for me and Paul to be best friends away from the show and have any kind of acceptable relationship on the show."

Like Carson, and unlike so many failed pretenders to the throne, the late-night talk show is David Letterman's true calling, his form of expression, and not just a job. "All I ever wanted to do is have a television show," he said. "And I've got one. So from that standpoint, I feel like I've succeeded. I also think *The Tonight Show* is the only other show I would do. I think once this show gets canceled or I get fired, you'll never see me again in another TV show of my own."

24

War at Midnight

The Tonight Show became the launching pad for many careers in all areas of entertainment. Most get their break on *Tonight* and have their own wonderful careers. A special handful get their break there and make late-night their lives. The latter group includes David Letterman, Jay Leno, and Joan Rivers. It was Rivers who, with husband Edgar as executive producer, went head-to-head with Carson.

From that first spot on the show in the '60s, there was some spark between Carson and Rivers. Carson was Rivers' father figure. "He handed me my career," she later said. Quickly she began winning fame and became as close to a regular on *The Tonight Show* as you could get. She accomplished what no one else was able to in 1983, she became Carson's exclusive guest host. Before Rivers, Fred de Cordova would have to hunt down different perspectives each night Carson was away. Finding guest hosts was more difficult than guests, because a guest need only be amusing ten, fifteen, twenty minutes; a guest host needed to maintain momentum for a full hour.

Joan Rivers changed all that, and a large part of de Cordova's headache was gone. "She was available, we leapt," he said. By serving as Carson's sole replacement, it kind of conferred on her the title of honorary "queen of the night." Carson and Rivers took midnight by storm; they counterbalanced each other.

Carson was deliberate, straightfoward. Rivers was brassy, impertinent, stirring things up. In a joke, Carson would land a solid jab; Rivers would slice away until there were ribbons left. "It is unlikely that any television personality, including Howard Cosell, has inspired more protest mail than Miss Rivers," explained de Cordova. "Our staff keeps a record of all the mail the program receives: the number of requests for autographed photos, gifts for Johnny, suggestions for guest appearances, cartoons and jokes, cassettes of 'talented' friends and acquaintances, and pro and con comments on our guests and guest hosts. The letters on Joan always ran twenty to one—against."

"Our personal relationship was curious," Rivers said of her years with Carson. "We saw each other socially maybe four times since 1972, when I moved to California, and then only in large groups. Our friendship existed entirely on-camera in front of America, and even then, during the commercial breaks, when the red light went off, we had nothing to say to each other beyond 'How's Edgar?,' 'Gee, doesn't the band sound great tonight'— and even the banalities lapsed after 30 seconds, Johnny sitting silent, drumming his pencil on the desk. When the red light went back on, magically we were like twins, winging on the same wavelength. I think we are both basically loners and terribly shy, both pretending to ourselves that the tremendous warmth and rapport we had on-camera extended to real life."

Rivers proved, however, to be a problematic guest host for the staid team of Carson and de Cordova. de Cordova had to hold her hand; he had to clear her monologue and her wardrobe. She was too daring, too quick to insult. More than that, she leaned *toward* the youth market. Too often her selection of guests did not meet with de Cordova's approval. When she jumped the *Tonight* ship, she had Cher, Elton John, Pee Wee Herman, and David Lee Roth her debut night, a guest list that would've had eightysomething de Cordova in a dead faint.

She said, "I gave him unwavering loyalty. Actually loyalty beyond intelligence. When Merv Griffin went up against Johnny on CBS in New York, I received all sorts of offers to appear on Merv's show. But I was the only one who would not go. During the past two years I was offered my own talk show on another network that said it would make me the queen of the network. Orion and Viacom wanted me for syndicated shows opposite Carson. I would have been set for life. When I said no, my advisers thought I'd had a lobotomy.

"I always swore I would never go up against Johnny. Loyalty is a fetish with me. There is little else except relationships in this world and, as one gets older, relationships become more intense, more special, more counted on—so I never wanted to do anything to hurt that man."

Not offending Carson went to extremes for Rivers. When Carson was breaking up with Joanna, Joanna ran into Rivers and asked if they could remain friends after the divorce. Rivers bluntly refused, saying that her relationship with Carson was more important.

Rivers began to feel she wasn't a valued member of the show, beyond the fact that she had to clear everything with de Cordova. "A lot of things were happening at NBC that did not instill confidence," Rivers explained. Usually, her *Tonight* contracts ran the same length as those of Carson. If Carson was on for a two year contract, Rivers was on for two years. In 1985, Carson signed for two years, but Rivers was only given one.

She said, "I had to face the fact that I was often taken for granted . . . . I held in my hand an NBC interoffice memo listing suggested successors to Johnny in case he did not renew his contract. My name was not on it. That told this insecure Jewish comic, 'Honey, you'd better think about new employment.'

"I was rarely included in the Carson 'family.' I was not even asked to the yearly Carson show party until ['86], when somebody told them, 'She would really, really like to come.'

"My first inkling that the network brass were not buddies came when I hosted the 1983 Emmy Awards with Eddie Murphy.

In the script there was a rough joke about James Watt, written by the Emmy staff. The network executives heard me say it during rehearsals and they laughed. In the show, I read the joke off the cue cards. But when the line created a furor in the press, NBC announced that it had been my ad-lib, my sin. The *Titanic* was going down, and NBC was jumping into the lifeboats ahead of the women and children."

This treatment sent Rivers the message that her future was elsewhere. Her manager Bill Sammeth had tried to open talks on a new NBC contract, and got the run-around for weeks. Finally NBC got back and stalled again. She thought about approaching Carson directly, but "we were constantly being ordered by his producers and his lawyer, 'You do not go to Johnny. You do not upset Johnny,'" she recalled.

It was NBC's hemming and hawing that gave Rivers pause to consider the offer that Fox Broadcasting put on her table. In the mid 1980s, Fox was assembling a "fourth network" out of independent stations around the country. Although Fox is doing well today with hits such as *The Simpsons* and *Married With Children*, they were having difficulty signing up new broadcast stations in the cable-conscious '80s.

They wanted a late-night program with Rivers to jumpstart the effort. With her connection to NBC so tenuous, she took the offer. "Now I can go for spontaneity, try for the excitement that comes from taking chances," Rivers said just before her *Late Show* premiered. "A talk show should be on the edge, suspenseful, a little bit dangerous. I want the show to be talked about, want sometimes to shock, want people to be rude or cry or storm off or come out drunk. That is what used to happen with Jack Paar, and people discussed the show the next day. Nowadays talk shows are oatmeal without sugar."

Ironically, while Rivers was preparing to jump to Fox, she was in the midst of a *Tonight Show* stint. She hadn't told Carson of her plan. She said, "I did not dare tell Johnny and burn that bridge until I had signed the Fox contract. I do not trust any deal until all the signatures are on the paper."

Carson heard the shocking news of Joan Rivers' move from NBC chief Brandon Tartikoff. It was the evening of Rivers' press conference announcing her shift to Fox. No sooner than Tartikoff had hung up, the phone rang again. It was de Cordova. Rivers and her husband Edgar had just sadly told the producer of their intention to leave. Another Carson phone rang. This time it was Rivers herself. "I'm not taking her call," Carson told de Cordova. "It was a little late in arriving . . . about three months late."

Rivers tried to reach her former boss again the next day. "I reached him from a wall phone in the Fox makeup room. I said, 'Johnny, I . . .' The phone went click. He had believed the worst without talking to me. In the midst of happiness and optimism, my grief gushed out. Pressing my forehead against the wall, I cried. Almost certainly he and I could never patch this up, could never put a piece of rubber over this split and pretend it had not happened. In that instant, a very old and crucial relationship passed away," Rivers said.

Apparently what insulted Carson was not that Rivers was doing the new show, but rather that she had not told him until it was almost too late. "A second-hand discovery that a member of your family has moved out of your home doesn't make for fun and celebrations," de Cordova said frankly. Like most everything that rankled him, Carson made public fun of Rivers and the phone call not taken on the show. Joking about former President Mikhail Gorbachev's problems in the former Soviet Union, Carson said, "It's all my fault. He called me . . . but I hung up on him."

When David Brenner, another *Tonight Show* bred comedian, attempted his own syndicated competition against Carson, Carson had wished Brenner all the best. Rivers conceded, "Obviously, I should have told Johnny earlier.

"The way Johnny found out about my new talk show was horrendous. I wanted to be the one to break the news to him—and had planned to do it first thing Tuesday morning, the day of the press conference. When I learned the news had been leaked to Johnny on Monday, the day I signed the contracts, I went into shock. All weekend I had been rehearsing and memorizing my little speech, saying, 'Johnny, it has nothing to do with you. It's the treatment I've been getting from everybody else.'"

Rivers had hoped to get the same send-off Brenner received before Carson pummeled Brenner into the ratings floor. "That is what I had wanted and planned," Rivers said, "sure that this parental figure would be proud and, when he heard my reasons, would say, 'I don't blame you, kiddo. I'll be on your first show.' I just believed that Johnny, so totally on top of the mountain, was the one person who would understand." Rivers and Carson evidently have not spoken since.

"Everyone on the show was scared to stay in contact with me. Ed McMahon was the only one who went over and kissed me and wished me well," Rivers said.

When *The Late Show* debuted, it captured the nation's attention. Fox only had 99 independents and six company-owned stations, hardly a match for NBC, yet she beat Carson's ratings in San Francisco and New York. It looked as if Rivers might be David to Carson's Goliath.

The strong opening night didn't lead to a long-term success. When Carson took over from Paar, he paced himself through thirty years. Rivers was a one-time bombshell that exploded and fizzled into nothing. The ratings slipped. She couldn't keep up her insolent veneer. As Carson biographer Laurence Leamer said, "She was *nice* to her guests, and it was often a bore."

Within a year, *The Late Show* was off. Fox tried the show with temporary hosts, but that was worse. "Joan joined the parade of those who fired and fell back," Fred de Cordova said of her battle with *The Tonight Show*. Her failure didn't make Carson feel any better. When the others before Rivers—Bishop, Cavett, Brenner, and Canadian Alan Thicke—all failed, Carson had them back on *The Tonight Show*, almost to say that he's big enough not to be concerned about their efforts. But Carson never asked Joan Rivers back.

Finding work after *The Late Show* was difficult. Only one television program would take her, *Hollywood Squares*. Her husband committed suicide and she had to put her life back together. She developed a syndicated morning talk show a couple of years later, *The Joan Rivers Show*, and has done well against her daylight competitors. That success hasn't gotten her a seat next to Carson.

25

Alex

Johnny Carson apparently met his fourth wife, Alexis Mass, as she strolled on the beach in front of his Malibu home. They soon began dating. She was born in Pittsburgh in 1950, her father a travelling salesman and her mother a housewife. "Alexis was born and grew up in Pittsburgh, and went to Mount Mercy Catholic School in Pennsylvania. She majored in art history and is very interested in art," said one Carson friend. Art appreciation is one of those things she shares with Carson.

"Alex is a good friend to Johnny. She never married before because she never found the right man. She really loves Johnny, and he really loves her," that friend continued.

After she graduated from school, she went to Boston and worked in state politics. Her former boss said, "She came in with a good resume and clearly was a lovely person. She had, in fact, a movie star quality. She worked out to be a perfect administrator— she would answer the phones and trouble-shoot for the governor. She had good skills and was great with people. She'd never get annoyed."

A former co-worker said of Mass, "Alexis was stunning looking . . . . She had a kind of Farrah Fawcett look with her mane of hair . . . and she clearly had an active social life . . . . She'd go tootling off to New York for weekends leaving us plebian folk on the sidelines saying, 'Wow!'"

"She was always talking about going out to California for a vacation," said her former boss. "I had a feeling about that. I told

her, 'If you go out to California, you'll never come back.' That's exactly what happened. She went out to California and fell in love with it. About a month after she returned, she announced she was moving there."

Mass relocated to the West Coast and found good jobs working as the personal assistant for department store and bank managers. She took many people by surprise with her relationship with Carson. She was an unknown when the gossip press began to report on their relationship in the mid '80s. They had been seeing Carson with Sally Fields and Loni Anderson, and were taken aback by this mysterious blonde.

Their relationship took people by surprise in another way. When she and Carson were becoming "serious," they began to look for an apartment together. "When they decided to take an apartment together," another Carson acquaintance explained, "Alexis went in and looked and asked if they could rent. The building managers at first said no, that the apartments were strictly for sale, not for rent. But finally they said yes because the building, in fact, was nearly empty, and it really wouldn't hurt to have additional tenants making it look lively.

"They showed her an apartment on the first floor. She like it and said, 'I'll bring my boyfriend back on Sunday to look at it.' And that Sunday she walks in with Johnny Carson!"

The couple decorated and moved in. Eventually Carson bought the apartment for $450,000. They were married in June, 1987. "His recent marriage to Alexis Mass came as no surprise to me," said Fred de Cordova. "Johnny had constantly indicated his happiness with their relationship and regularly talked of their similar tastes and reactions and evaluations. In the past Johnny has always paid for his thrills—I feel those days are over."

Carson and his new wife share a similar temperament for quiet and privacy. "I think Alexis is very good for Johnny," said the wife of a *Tonight Show* executive. "She gives him a center and focus and doesn't need to be a separate personality or star.

Alexis is content to be a consort. Joanna wanted to be a star in her own right."

The "center and focus" Mrs. Carson gives her husband is security, a freedom that has allowed him to pursue his first love with all his heart, *The Tonight Show.*

26

Johnny Carson's Primetime

Carson celebrated twenty-five years on *The Tonight Show* in 1987. Despite observations that he wasn't "hip" enough, that he wasn't in touch with a younger audience, he was bigger than ever. It was an entertainment milestone equalled in magnitude by few. Like each previous year, the anniversary show of October 1 was a primetime gala, but each landmark brought greater legend and tribute on the anniversary, first the ten year, fifteen, and then twenty. The twenty-fifth surpassed all of them.

"Johnny Carson stepped from behind the multicolored curtain wearing a tuxedo," said Laurence Leamer, a Carson biographer who attended the taping of the twentyfifth anniversary special. "The five hundred screaming guests rose from their seats in Studio 1. They clapped, screamed, whistled, and hooted exuberantly. Johnny walked forward to a star marked on the studio floor. Carl 'Doc' Severinsen salaamed, twirling his hand downward from his forehead. McMahon paid homage too, pressing his hands together and bowing if to a royal personage.

"The camera panned across the audience, capturing snapshots of middle America. A family from Louisiana. A couple from Pennsylvania. A retired man from New Jersey. Two sisters from Seattle. Most of the audience had come to southern California on vacations. They had made this pilgrimage to *The Tonight Show* as important a part of their itineraries as Disneyland or the Universal Studio tour.

1962-63   1963-64   1964-65   1965-66   1966-67

1967-68   1968-69   1969-70   1970-71   1971-72

1972-73   1973-74

1974-75   1975-76

1976-77   1977-78   1978-79   1979-80   1980-81

1981-82   1982-83   1983-84   1984-85   1985-86

"This morning, October 1, 1987, close to a hundred of the guests had been standing in line at the NBC studios in Burbank waiting for tickets when a major earthquake hit Los Angeles. Even that didn't dislodge them.

"The applause didn't end, but rose from crescendo to crescendo. He had become a fixture of American life, a part of the cultural furniture. This evening alone, over 21 million people were watching the show."

Carson appeared and began his monologue. "People are not used to seeing me in primetime," he quipped. "Imagine President Reagan tuning in now and saying to Nancy, 'Well, it's eleven-thirty, I should have been asleep two hours ago.'

"Would you have believed twenty-five years ago that now, today, in '87, we'd be seeing condom ads on television?" Johnny observed, with that famous surprised-Carson tone. "Now the next time you hear Ed say, 'On your way home, pick up a six pack,' he may not be referring to Budweiser."

Carson ended his monologue, and said, "Thank you for being with us," before they cut to a commercial.

1987 marked the era of a stable Johnny Carson. His battles with the network were over; he no longer had to fight to be treated like the entertainment royalty he was. The notorious drinking bouts that threw him onto the covers of scandal sheets had ended. His ex-wives were behind him, leaving behind nothing more than alimony checks. By all accounts his current marriage with Alex Mass was fine. In fact, Alex had contributed to Carson's happy tranquility. She had no inclination to throw Carson into the social set, so he was finally able to live the successful, but private life he had always wanted.

1992 would have marked Johnny Carson's thirtieth anniversary on *The Tonight Show*, another milestone. Instead, it became a different landmark altogether, the year of his retirement. To most people's surprise, he announced his intended retirement in the summer of '91. He said he would stay until May, '92 and call it quits. The October '91 twenty-ninth anniversary special on primetime took a plaintive tone with the impending end. The special garnered higher ratings than the show had ever seen. It was worse that Carson's "end" went on for almost a year. Toward the last few months, studio tickets for shows that Carson hosted went faster than ever.

In Carson's final weeks on the show, one *Time* journalist noted, "Now, as the long-awaited finale draws near, a show that has always depended for its appeal on the offhand, the spontaneous and ephemeral is acquiring the air of great moment."

"A part of Americana is leaving," said one staff member. If de Cordova and his staff had had headaches getting celebrities to fit the show into their schedules before, they had to fend them off in '91 and '92. They all clamored for their last shot with Carson. Elizabeth Taylor made her first appearance on the show ever in 1992, thanking Carson for "thirty years of brilliant entertainment."

The attention paid to all of Carson's years seemed daunting to his come-lately competitors. "I've been doing this for thirty shows, he's been doing it for thirty years. It's a tough gig, and he still looks like he enjoys it," said Dennis Miller, the *Saturday Night Live* alumnus who recently got his own late-night show.

It was also a last chance for viewers to see the characters Carson made famous. The show's writers pulled psychic Carnac, salesman letch Art Fern, bigot Floyd Turbo, vampire El Moldo, even old Aunt Blabby for last visits.

The departure took on greater significance when most of the Carson-era staff said they would leave with him; Ed McMahon, Severinsen, producer Fred de Cordova and others would all turn over the late-night court to a crown prince. "In a way, it's agonizing," said Severinsen. "The ending is going on and on. The pain is being extended—and there *is* pain."

The other "great moment" for The Tonight Show was the decision of who would sit in that chair after Carson.

27

Crowning the New King

When Johnny Carson leaves *The Tonight Show*, his regulars, including McMahon, are leaving with him. It is truely a changing of the guard.

NBC waited two weeks after Carson's announcement to anoint a new host for *The Tonight Show*. The two major contenders were permanent guest host Jay Leno and guest host alumnus David Letterman. Two years earlier, when asked if he would consider taking over *The Tonight Show*, Letterman said, "I guess of course I would. But I think ultimately I would be happy just to be considered."

Letterman was considered, but most figured he would remain with his own successful program. Leno had received good notices during his tenure as Carson's exclusive stand-in. "It's the passing of an era," explained Rod Perth, CBS' vice president of late-night entertainment. "And with any change in the sort of dominance that Carson had over the years, there's bound to be a backwash of uncertainty. This is a choice they're going to have to live with for a long time, and their affiliates are really breathing down their neck to keep the franchise alive."

NBC made the declaration that Leno would be the one stepping into the breach. "I like to look back at the history of hosts and say, 'Gee, it's my turn not to drop the ball," Leno said after the decision was made. "It's like being given the crown jewels. You hold on to them and make sure nobody steals them. Then you pass them on to somebody else."

The tabloids began to play up a Leno/Letterman feud over the decision, although the two have admired each other for years. Letterman said that Leno was not a "show business weasel." One

television critic, however, wrote, "if *Tonight* suddenly spring a serious leak in the post-Carson era, who else would NBC dare turn to?"

Helen Kushnick, Leno's manager for eighteen years and executive producer of *The Tonight Show* after Fred de Cordova leaves in the mass Carson-gang exodus, defends Leno, saying, "It's like the John Houseman line. He's done it the old fashioned way. He's *earned* it."

Carson gave Leno his own seal of approval, while not leaving Letterman out of the scene. "I wish Jay all the success in the world," Carson said after NBC's decision went public. "He's a bright young performer, and I think along with David Letterman, who has proven his staying power the past ten years, NBC will have a great late-night lineup."

Leno returned the compliment in kind. "Johnny's the best at what he does," Leno said after he was named the crown-prince of late-night. "He set the standard and his remarkable career will never be repeated."

After proving his success on *Tonight* as Carson's permanent stand-in, Leno began getting the same offers Joan Rivers once got; his own late-night show opposite Carson. Unlike Rivers, Leno didn't feel the need to grab the offer. "I've sort of been a good soldier," Leno said. "[The network] sort of gave me an indication that when Johnny was ready to retire, this would go into action. It was a preparation. They'd say, 'Can you do this?' But I've worked Caesar's in Las Vegas since 1977. I've had the same manager for 18 years. When I go somewhere, it's to stay. It's a bit like living together for five years and then deciding to get married. I like things that have a sense of history."

Leno himself has a sense of history. He is a Boston native, grew up there, and went to Emerson College there, too. He's the son of an Italian insurance salesman and a mother who came to America from Scotland when she was twelve. Leno calls his father "the funniest guy in the office." By the time he was a sophomore in college, he was driving to New York City on weekends to try out at comedy clubs. After graduation he worked comedy wherever he could, rock concerts, Playboy clubs, and strip joints.

He moved to California in the early '70s to make it in the comic business. He met Mavis Nicholson at the Comedy Store in Hollywood; they later married. "I don't do wife jokes," Leno said. The other event that would change Leno's life happened at the Improvisation in '75. Johnny Carson was in the audience, and was impressed. He gave Leno a few pointers and invited him onto *The Tonight Show*. Jay Leno's first appearance on the show was on March 2, 1977. Leno came on last, after Burt Reynolds and Diana Ross.

Leno went back to *Tonight* several times, but struggled more each time. He went back to stand-up in clubs, then made his television come-back on David Letterman's show. He was more at ease with Letterman; Carson made him nervous. Leno returned to *The Tonight Show* more confident in the shadow of the King of Midnight and won the exclusive guest host job in '87, replacing Joan Rivers.

Jay Leno may be the ideal successor to midnight's throne. He embodies the spirit of *The Tonight Show*, not just that of Johnny Carson. Leno, more than cynical, sarcastic Letterman, can hold Carson's audience with his open affability, but he has the appeal to gain a wider one. Carson is very Midwestern; Leno brings a more urban feel. Carson's audience was mostly WASPs; Leno attracts ethnic viewers. Most importantly, Leno attracts the elusive 18-to-34-year-old viewers. He's hip without putting off the non-hip. As guest host, his ratings nearly matched Carson's. Comedian friend Jerry Seinfeld said, "His uniqueness is that he is sophisticated and broad at the same time, so hip and so ordinary."

Leno's approach to comedy and monologues is different from Carson's. Johnny's hallmark was the lewd sex joke that comes off funny, but not dirty. Leno doesn't do much sex material. His monologues arise from current events and politics. Carson divided his jibes among all politicians, not revealing his own opinions. Fred de Cordova once said that in the twenty years they worked together, he could never tell if Carson was a Democrat or Republican. Leno is different. As one journalist said, "When he says, 'Pat Buchanan is the thinking man's David Duke,' he says it to be funny, but he also means it." Leno is quick to point out that he isn't trying to be a funny, liberal, George Will. "Political implies ideological, and my comedy is not ideological."

Carson has been poking fun at his own age, and the obvious aging of the original Carson *Tonight Show*. Comedian Don Rickles was a *Tonight* staple for years, but now has little place on the show. Rickles made an appearance after Carson announced his departure. "What are you going to do now? Where are you going to go now?" Rickles asked Carson.

Carson pointedly deadpanned, "The question is, where are *you* going to go?"

All eyes focus on Leno to keep *The Tonight Show* alive without the Carson legend in an era of increasing competition. He will bring changes. The signature theme, written by Paul Anka three decades ago, will be dropped in favor of a contemporary tune. "It's like hearing 'Thanks for the Memory' and saying, 'So where's Bob Hope?'" Leno said.

Jazz great Branford Marsalis will replace Doc Severinsen as bandleader. Pundits suggested Leno abandon the well-known orchestra in favor of a Letterman-like rock band. Leno wisely turned that down. He believes the orchestra will add class and quiet continuity.

There was no greater speculation than who would succeed Ed McMahon as sidekick. Media watchers predicted *Saturday Night Live* star Dana Carvey would be the best candidate. Leno doesn't believe a sidekick is obligatory. He's forgoing a partner altogether to do it his way. There will be other changes as Leno settles into his throne.

He sees his future clearly by looking at forty years of television history. And he has a clear vision of his place in the world.

"When you think of some of the horrible thing's this country's been through, the assassination of John F. Kennedy and Martin Luther King, the Vietnam years, the fact that Johnny was able to get up night after night and find comedy in the day's events or find some way to make people laugh, that's a hard thing to do," Leno explained. "Let *Nightline* handle the crises and Donohue ask the probing questions. On *Tonight* you want to have the lighter side. I hope it never changes."

Bibliography

Besides the assistance or interviews from such people as Steve Allen and Jack Paar, many sources were used in researching this book. Several newspaper and magazine articles past and present from publications such as Time, Newsweek, the Saturday Evening Post, the Boston Globe, the Los Angeles Times, the Chicago Tribune and the New York Times. In addition, the following were used:

Allen, Steve, Hi-Ho, Steverino, New York: Barricade Books, 1992.

Allen, Steve, Mark It and Strike It, New York: Hillman Books, 1961.

Corkery, Paul, Carson: The Unauthorized Biography, New York: Randt and Co., 1987.

De Cordova, Fred, Johnny Came Lately, New York: Simon and Schuster, 1987.

Leamer, Laurence, King of the Night, New York: William Morrow and Co., 1989.

Metz, Robert, The Tonight Show, Chicago: Playboy Press, 1980.

Paar, Jack, I Kid You Not, Boston: Little, Brown, and Co., 1960.

Paar, Jack, My Saber is Bent, New York: Simon and Schuster, 1961.

Tennis, Craig, Johnny Tonight!, New York: Pocket Books, 1980.

THE HISTORY OF TREK

The Complete Story of Star Trek from Original Conception to its Effects on Millions of Lives Across the World

James Van Hise

- *Star Trek VI*, the last Trek movie to star the original crew, will be released this winter
- By the author of *The Trek Crew Book* and *The Best of Enterprise Incidents: The Magazine for Star Trek Fans*

This book celebrates the 25th anniversary of the first "Star Trek" television episode and traces the history of the show that has become an enduring legend—even non-Trekkies can quote specific lines and characters from the original television series. *The History of Trek* chronicles "Star Trek" from its start in 1966 to its cancellation in 1969; discusses the lean years when "Star Trek" wasn't shown on television but legions of die-hard fans kept interest in it alive; covers the sequence of five successful movies (and includes the upcoming sixth one); and reviews "The Next Generation" television series, now entering its sixth season.

Perhaps no series in the history of television has had as much written about it as "Star Trek," but fans continue to snap up books and magazines about their favorite show. When the series first appeared on television in the 1960s, a book was already available chronicling its creation. And after the show was dropped three years later, people continued to write about it, actually increasing attention to the show until it returned in the form of a $40 million feature film in 1979.

Complete with photographs, *The History of Trek* reveals the origins of the first series in interviews with the original cast and creative staff. It also takes readers behind the scenes of all six Star Trek movies, offers a wealth of Star Trek trivia, and speculates on what the future may hold. A must for Trekkies, science fiction fans, and television and film buffs.

James Van Hise is the author of numerous books on entertainment, including *Batmania* and *The 25th Anniversary Lost in Space Tribute*. He lives in San Diego, CA.

$14.95, Trade paper, ISBN 1-55698-309-3
Television/Film, 25 B&W photos, 160pp, 8⅜ x 10⅞
Pioneer Books

TWENTY-FIFTH ANNIVERSARY TREK TRIBUTE

James Van Hise

- The Star Trek phenomenon is celebrating its 25th anniversary
- Written by the author of *The Trek Crew Book* and *The Best of Enterprise Incidents: The Magazine for Star Trek Fans*

Taking a close-up look at the amazing Star Trek story, this book traces the history of the show that has become an enduring legend. James Van Hise chronicles the series from 1966 to its cancellation in 1969, through the years when only the fans kept it alive, and on to its unprecedented revival. He offers a look at its latter-day blossoming into an animated series, a sequence of five movies (with a sixth in preparation) that has grossed over $700 million, and the offshoot "The Next Generation" TV series, which will be entering its fifth season as Star Trek celebrates 25 years of trekking.

Complemented with a variety of photographs and graphics, the text traces the broken path back from cancellation, the revelation of the show's afterlife in conventions, and its triumphant return in the wide screen in *Star Trek: The Movie*. He also looks at such spin-off phenomena as the more than 100 Star Trek books in print—many of them bestsellers—and the 50 million video-cassettes on the market.

The author gives readers a tour of the memorials at the Smithsonian and the Movieland Wax Museums, lets them witness Leonard Nimoy get his star on the Hollywood Walk of Fame in 1985, and takes them behind the scenes of the motion-picture series and TV's "The Next Generation." The concluding section examines the future of Star Trek beyond its 25th anniversary.

James Van Hise who has authored such comics as *The Real Ghostbusters* and *Fright Night*, serves as publisher/editor of the highly acclaimed *Midnight Grafitti* and is the author of numerous nonfiction works, including *The Trek Crew Book*, *The Best of Enterprise Incidents*, *The Dark Shadows Tribute*, and *Batmania*. He lives in San Diego, CA.

$14.95, Trade paper, ISBN 1-55698-290-9
TV/Movies, 50 B&W photos, line drawings, maps, and charts throughout, 196pp, 8⅜ x 10⅞
Pioneer Books

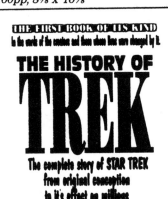

THE FIRST BOOK OF ITS KIND
Is the work of the reviews and those whose lives were changed by it

THE HISTORY OF
TREK
The complete story of STAR TREK from original conception to its effect on millions of lives across the world.
JAMES VAN HISE

TREK 25
CELEBRATION
By James Van Hise

Couch Potato Inc.

Las Vegas, NV 89130

TREK

The Next Generation

James Van Hise

● The *Star Trek* phenomenon celebrates its 25th anniversary as the new television series enters its fifth season

T hey said it wouldn't last, and, after its cancellation in 1969, it looked as if it wouldn't. But the fans refused to let it die and now *Star Trek* is thriving as never before. The *Next Generation* television series—entering its fifth year—continues the adventure. This book reveals the complete story behind the new series, the development of each major character, and gives plans for the future.

James Van Hise is publisher editor of *Midnight Graffiti* and has written numerous books, including *The 25th Annniversary Lost in Space Tribute*.

   $14.95, Trade paper. ISBN 1-55698-305-0
Television, B&W photos, 164pp. 8⅜ x 10⅞

Pioneer Books

THE COMPLETE
LOST IN SPACE
Written by John Peel

The complete guide to every single episode of LOST IN SPACE including profiles of every cast member and character.

The most exhaustive book ever written about LOST IN SPACE.

$19.95...220 pages

Las Vegas, NV 89130   (702)658-209

IT'S A BIRD, IT'S A PLANE
Written by James Van Hise

Few actors have so completely captured the public's imagination that when the name of the character he or she portrays is mentioned, that actor immediately comes to mind. Sean Connery is James Bond. Basil Rathbone is Sherlock Holmes. Clayton Moore is The Lone Ranger. And for 39 years George Reeves has been Superman! IT'S A BIRD, IT'S A PLANE examines the Superman television series, covering its 104 episodes in minute detail. Author James Van Hise provides a complete episode guide, interviews with Reeves' co-stars Noel Neill (Lois Lane), Jack Larson (Jimmy Olsen) and Robert Shayne (Inspector Henderson). In addition, the text includes complete cast biographies, a super-Superman quiz and a look at the George Reeves movie serial, THE ADVENTURES OF SIR GALAHAD, providing a guide to all fifteen chapters.

It's a bird...it's a plane...no, it's the greatest Superman book ever!

$14.95.................124 pages
Black and White Illustrations Throughout
ISBN#1-55698-201-1

IT'S A BIRD...
IT'S A PLANE...
NO IT'S THE...
TELEVISION
ADVENTURES OF
SUPERMAN

BY JAMES VAN HISE AND JOHN FIELD

$14.95/$19.95 CANADA   ISBN#1-55698-201-1   SCHUSTER AND SCHUSTER

The Green Hornet
Written by James Van Hise

Batman was not the only superhero television series to air in the 1960s. Its creators also brought ABC's THE GREEN HORNET, which starred Van Williams as the Green Hornet with martial arts superstar Bruce Lee as his sidekick, Kato, to the screen.

A guide to every episode of the television series, with actor and character profiles make this a complete look at this unique super hero.

$14.95...........120 pages
Color Cover, Black and White Interior Photos
SPECIAL OFFER: A limited edition volume combining the books on THE GREEN HORNET television series and the movie serial. This two-in-one book is only $16.95!

Boring, But Necessary Ordering Information!

Payment:
All orders must be prepaid by check or money order. Do not send cash. All payments must be made in US funds only.

Shipping:
We offer several methods of shipment for our product. Sometimes a book can be delayed if we are temporarily out of stock. You should note on your order whether you prefer us to ship the book as soon as available or send you a merchandise credit good for other goodies or send you your money back immediately.

Postage is as follows:

Normal Post Office: For books priced under $10.00—for the first book add $2.50. For each additional book under $10.00 add $1.00. (This is per indidividual book priced under $10.00. Not the order total.) For books priced over $10.00—for the first book add $3.25. For each additional book over $10.00 add $2.00.(This is per individual book priced over $10.00, not the order total.)
These orders are filled as quickly as possible. Shipments normally take 2 or 3 weeks, but allow up to 12 weeks for delivery.

Special UPS 2 Day Blue Label Rush Service or Priority Mail(Our Choice). Special service is available for desperate Couch Potatoes. These books are shipped within 24 hours of when we receive the order and should normally take 2 to 3 days to get from us to you.
For the first RUSH SERVICE book under $10.00 add $5.00. For each additional 1 book under $10.00 add $1.75. (This is per individual book priced under $10.00, not the order total.)
For the first RUSH SERVICE book over $10.00 add $7.00 For each additional book over $10.00 add $4.00 per book.(This is per individual book priced over $10.00, not the order total.)

Canadian shipping rates add 20% to the postage total.
Foreign shipping rates add 50% to the postage total.
All Canadian and foreign orders are shipped either book or printed matter.
Rush Service is not available.

DISCOUNTS!DISCOUNTS!
Because your orders keep us in business we offer a discount to people that buy a lot of our books as our way of saying thanks. On orders over $25.00 we give a 5% discount. On orders over $50.00 we give a 10% discount. On orders over $100.00 we give a 15% discount. On orders over over $150.00 we giver a 20 % discount.

Please list alternates when possible.

Please state if you wish a refund or for us to backorder an item if it is not in stock.

100% satisfaction guaranteed.
We value your support. You will receive a full refund as long as the copy of the book you are not happy with is received back by us in reasonable condition. No questions asked, except we would like to know how we failed you. Refunds and credits are given as soon as we receive back the item you do not want.

Please have mercy on Phyllis and carefully fill out this form in the neatest way you can. Remember, she has to read a lot of them every day and she wants to get it right and keep you happy! You may use a duplicate of this order blank as long as it is clear. Please don't forget to include payment! And remember, we love repeat friends.

____Trek: The Lost Years $12.95   ISBN#1-55698-220-8

____Trek: The Next Generation $14.95   ISBN#1-55698-305-0

____Trek: Twentyfifth Anniversary Celebration $14.95   ISBN#1-55698-290-9

____The Making Of The Next Generation $14.95   ISBN#1-55698-219-4

____The Best Of Enterprise Incidents: The Mag For Star Trek Fans $9.95 ISBN#1-55698-231-3

____The History Of Trek $14.95   ISBN#1-55698-309-3

____Trek Fan's Handbook $9.95   ISBN#1-55698-271-2

____The Trek Crewbook $9.95   ISBN#1-55698-257-7

____The Man Between The Ears: Star Trek's Leonard Nimoy $14.95   ISBN#1-55698-304-2

____The Doctor And The Enterprise $9.95   ISBN#1-55698-218-6

____The Lost In Space Tribute Book $14.95   ISBN#1-55698-226-7

____The Complete Lost In Space $19.95

____The Lost In Space Tech Manual $14.95

____Doctor Who: The Complete Baker Years $19.95   ISBN#1-55698-147-3

____The Doctor Who Encyclopedia: The Baker Years $19.95 ISBN#1-55698-160-0

____Doctor Who: The Pertwee Years $19.95   ISBN#1-55698-212-7

____Number Six: The Prisoner Book $14.95   ISBN#1-55698-158-9

____Gerry Anderson: Supermarionation $14.95

____The L.A. Lawbook $14.95   ISBN#1-55698-295-X

____The Rockford Phile $14.95   ISBN#1-55698-288-7

____Cheers: Where Everybody Knows Your Name $14.95   ISBN#1-55698-291-7

____It's A Bird It's A Plane $14.95   ISBN#1-55698-201-1

____The Green Hornet Book $16.95 Edition

____How To Draw Art For Comic Books $14.95   ISBN#1-55698-254-2

____How To Create Animation $14.95   ISBN#1-55698-285-2

____Rocky & The Films Of Stallone $14.95   ISBN#1-55698-225-9

____The New Kids Block $9.95   ISBN#1-55698-242-9

____Monsterland Fearbook $14.95

____The Unofficial Tale Of Beauty And The Beast $14.95   ISBN#1-55698-261-5

____The Hollywood Death Book $14.95   ISBN#1-55698-307-7

____The Addams Family Revealed $14.95   ISBN#1-55698-300-X

____The Dark Shadows Tribute Book $14.95   ISBN#1-55698-234-8

____Stephen King & Clive Barker: An Illustrated Guide $14.95 ISBN#1-55698-253-4

____Stephen King & Clive Barker: Illustrated Guide II $14.95 ISBN#1-55698-310-7

____The Fab Films Of The Beatles $14.95   ISBN#1-55698-244-5

____Paul McCartney: 20 Years On His Own $9.95   ISBN#1-55698-263-1

_____Yesterday: My Life With the Beatles $14.95   ISBN#1-55698-292-5

_____Forty Years At Night: The Tonight Show Story   ISBN#1-55698-308-5 $14.95

_____The Films Of Elvis: The Magic Lives On $14.95   ISBN#1-55698-223-2

_____Batmania $14.95   ISBN#1-55698-252-6

_____Batmania II $14.95   ISBN#1-55698-315-8

_____The Phantom Serials $16.95

_____Batman Serials $16.95

_____Batman & Robin Serials $16.95

_____The Complete Batman & Robin Serials $19.95

_____The Green Hornet Serials $16.95

_____The Flash Gordon Serials Part 1 $16.95

_____The Flash Gordon Serials Part 2 $16.95

_____The Shadow Serials $16.95

_____Blackhawk Serials $16.95

_____Serial Adventures $14.95   ISBN#1-55698-236-4

_____Encyclopedia Of Cartoon Superstars $14.95   ISBN#1-55698-269-0

_____The Woody Allen Encyclopedia $14.95   ISBN#1-55698-303-4

_____The Gunsmoke Years $14.95   ISBN#1-55698-221-6

_____The Wild Wild West $14.95   ISBN#1-55698-162-7

_____Who Was That Masked Man $14.95   ISBN#1-55698-227-5

_____The Man Who Created Star Trek $14.95   ISBN #1-55698-318-2

_____Trek: The Making of the Movies $14.95   ISBN#1-55698-313-1

NAME:_____

STREET:_____

CITY:_____

STATE:_____

ZIP:_____

TOTAL:_____ SHIPPING_____

SEND TO: Couch Potato, Inc. 5715 N. Balsam Rd., Las Vegas, NV 89130